# Our India

**Advance Praise for *Our India***

'Captain Gopinath has led many lives. As an Army man, an organic farmer, a politician who contested two elections, and a significant contributor to the airline industry. The wide-ranging collections of essays in this book, on enterprise, economy, politics, governance, societal issues, etc. are witty, vivid, and packed with personal anecdotes. He is truly a man of the new renaissance, and this book is a must-read!'

– Nandan Nilekani, chairman and co-founder, Infosys; and founding chairman, UIDAI

'Captain Gopinath's *Our India* strives to spur national discussion on issues critical to our times and is a forthright voice of reason in a world that is drowned in cacophony.'

– Kiran Mazumder-Shaw, chairperson, Biocon

'This book by Captain Gopinath, citizen extraordinaire, reflects the views of a concerned Indian. As citizens, we need to express our views freely on major issues concerning the country's future, so that our elected representatives reflect our views in Parliament when they pass laws. His views on industry, aviation, the economy, politics, society, etc. are studied, and based on his life's experience and a deep understanding of modern issues. A must-read for all who are concerned about making our representative democracy work better.'

– T.V. Mohandas Pai, chairman, Aarin Capital Partners

'A brilliant example of the power of words to inform, energise, and persuade.'

– Kunal Basu, author and academic

CAPTAIN
G.R. GOPINATH

# Our India

## REFLECTIONS ON A NATION BETWIXT AND BETWEEN

HarperCollins *Publishers* India

First published in India in English by HarperCollins *Publishers* 2022
4th Floor, Tower A, Building No. 10, Phase II, DLF Cyber City,
Gurugram, Haryana – 122002
www.harpercollins.co.in

2 4 6 8 10 9 7 5 3 1



P-ISBN: 978-93-9440-715-2
E-ISBN: 978-93-9440-716-9



Typeset in 11/13.8 Minion Pro Regular at
Manipal Digital Systems, Manipal

Printed and bound at
Thomson Press (India) Ltd

MIX
Paper
FSC FSC® C010615

This book is produced from independently certified FSC® paper
to ensure responsible forest management.

*To all the faceless farmers, soldiers in forbidding and remote areas, small entrepreneurs, migrant and health workers toiling in the shadows, who are the true engine of the economy and backbone of the nation.*

# Contents

# Foreword

When, over six decades ago, I was at school, I found most of my textbooks a burden to bear and a chore to study. With one exception: Minoo R.Masani's *Our India*. First published in 1940, when its author was of the socialist persuasion, the book sold 500,000 copies. It was reprinted in 1953, by which time the world had been through World War II and the India that Masani had written about in 1940 had been through a trauma – Partition, and a triumph – Freedom. It was a book for children, essentially, but grown-ups profited from its carefully presented facts and figures about India, her land and its resources, her people, and their problems. And, in the 1953 edition, which we read at school, it suggested solutions, clearly but gently. And in a new preface for the new edition, the author said with pardonable confidence: "*Our India* may claim that it has played a small part as a pioneer in making India planning-minded and in preparing the way for the Five-Year Plan on which the country is now launched. The dream of yesteryear is thus on the way to becoming reality." The new edition retained the illustrations by C.H.G.Moorhouse in the original. I remember those illustrations even after all the intervening years have dimmed many recollections and dulled many a school-day memory.

Reading the pages of Capt. Gopinath's manuscript for the book with the same alluring title, I thought I would Google Masani's book to refresh my recollection of the book, and *lo,* there it was, available online, page after page, drawing after drawing, exactly as I had known it in school. All the words came ringing back, as did the sketches, each character in it, each line and shade, dusting time off my brain. But I also found in the preface now, what I as a school kid had glossed over: the author's handsome acknowledgment of other authors and books, which included Wadia's Geology of India, Ram Manohar Lohia's *India in Figures,* Hivale, and Elwin's *Songs of the Forest.* Among the individuals he acknowledged were the economist Professor M.L. Dantwala and the poetess Sarojini Naidu "for her encouragement and interest."

Capt. Gopinath's *Our India,* is an altogether different kind of book. It is meant for study and reflection by mature citizens of India and beyond. But it shares with its namesake of nearly seventy years ago this: It describes realities with great accuracy, with veracity. In other words, the truth. And it does so not to defend or to lament, not to justify or to offend but to suggest amelioration, rectification, redemption. And where the matter may be said to be 'out of hand,' to say as much but without the feeling that can be best expressed with the Tamil exclamation '*Ayyo!*' – a cry of hopelessness. Capt. Gopinath, like Minoo Masani, gives us nuggets from the writings of great authors, Indian and non-Indian. He does so with the same ease with which a weaver of Kanchipuram silk working on his loom introduces into the warp strands of glittering brocade, organically, and integrally to enrich the weave. And yet, in a remarkable facet of his style, he does so without making the quotations or references look like foreign matter. They flow into the narrative as gently as the gleaming gold does in the Kanchipuram yarn.

Not many connected with flying and flying machines can write with Capt. Gopinath's flair. But no one, I am sure, can write about the Tatas' great date with flying, bringing in Christopher Marlowe and Walt Disney into the proceedings. Or on his own experience of flying 'a small nine-seater Swiss Pilatus aircraft' from Cape Town, South Africa to Bombay, bringing right into the story, nothing more different and yet nothing more fitting than Charles Dickens' *Oliver Twist.* His narrations on matters as starkly contemporary as lockdowns and suchlike have William Shakespeare and Napoleon Bonaparte, Bertrand Russell and Adolf Hitler, Albert Camus, and Josef Stalin populate them.

This book is a compilation of the writings of a highly widely-read man who writes as he speaks, speaks as he thinks, and thinks with utter honesty. A reader of non-fiction prose cannot wish for more. If like classical Indian music, quality writing has to have a rasa, then Capt. Gopinath is the rasa of *Ananda*. There is discernible through the pages of the compilation a smile, sometimes wistful, sometimes playful, but not for a moment scornful. It has the humour of the 'knowing innocent'. The life-sketch of R.K.Laxman is the Prince of the book. It not just smiles and makes the reader do so but crackles with laughter, of the truest Laxman kind. If not the highest, then surely one of the truest forms of it is that which is aimed at oneself. Gopinath's descriptions of himself employ the sharpest witticisms. To write on serious and even grave matters without taking oneself seriously is a rare and redemptive gift.

Coming through rifts in the happy cloud of Capt. Gopinath's sensibility is a beam of pathos. Capt. Gopinath's essay on the late 'Coffee Café Day' Siddhartha is a profoundly moving document. It is no part of a foreword's remit to give away the contents of the book. But I have not been able to refrain from parting the curtain over some of the essentialities of its pages. I have done so with concern over the human condition which is at the core of the author's writing. He writes as a soldier and as a patriot but as one who does not flinch from speaking the bitter truth about us as a people and as Indians.

I do not doubt that like its predecessor namesake, this book will have a salience well beyond the year of its first publication and be turned to for its very distinct qualities.

Capt. Gopinath's *Our India* is a work of, and for the small truths of life that go into the making of that capital letter which so resembles Christ's Cross – T.

Gopalkrishna Gandhi
Bengaluru
24 April 2022

# Introduction

Capt. GR Gopinath is full of surprises; few would have expected a former army captain to be a political candidate for elected office, a serial entrepreneur, a sericulturist, an aviation pioneer, and an author to boot. And now this once-and-(maybe)-future entrepreneur has emerged as an interesting voice in the media, commenting on a variety of issues with the same panache he brought to his best-known business venture, Air Deccan. As you will discover when you go through the pages of this collection of opinion pieces, published over the years in a variety of media outlets, he is a gifted storyteller, he offers business insights when you don't expect them, and writes with the conviction of someone who speaks his mind. What he offers, therefore, is not profundity but reader connection.

Short pieces written for the media don't usually age well, and therefore are not necessarily the best material between the covers of a book that is meant to have longer-term value. But there are always some pieces that have stood the test of time, especially those borne out of personal experience. Inevitably, these are interspersed with commentary on immediate events, pieces that are rough cuts rather than polished work. So the reader naturally has to pick and choose what they might find interesting.

What I found arresting was the slightly hair-raising account of how Capt. Gopinath was negotiating simultaneously, with not just one or two but three different leading businessmen to find a partner for his low-cost airline, Deccan Aviation—as a fourth sought to enter the fray. And since business in India is never unmixed with politics, you find politicians phoning up to intercede on behalf of one potential investor or the other while professing not to be putting pressure. As we all know business in India is never without its twists and turns, you have term sheets that are signed but then expire, suitors who are negotiating simultaneously with Gopinath and also a rival airline, and eventually, a deal that sadly, fails to save the airline. Talk about flying by the seat of your pants!

Among the other engaging pieces are his encounters with people as varied as R.K. Laxman, Pandit Jasraj, and Girish Karnad. Capt. Gopinath is not without self-deprecating humour. In one instance, he says (and one can imagine his laugh as he says it) that his cheques were flying faster than his aircraft! Earlier in life, while in the army, he helped a young Muslim girl with whom he had had a brief romantic interest escape from her parents' home. He ponders how that harmless escapade might have ended up in today's more charged environment. Why even his commanding officer let him off lightly!

More seriously, he discusses how India's business environment is needlessly spoilt by governments by tax terrorism, he offers the simple insight that a shop cannot do good business in a bad neighbourhood. When commenting on the needlessly complicated goods and services tax (where a paratha is deemed to not be a flatbread because it is layered, and therefore, taxed at 18 percent instead of 5 percent), he offers a delightful American aphorism: *keep it simple, stupid!* Or KISS. He also recounts a story once told to him by Ramakrishna Hegde, while he was the minister of commerce in Delhi, about how rule-bound India's bureaucratic gate-keepers could be, by giving the example of how a guard at a well-known Hindu temple asked some foreign visitors to take off their shoes. When it was pointed out to him that they were already barefoot since they had left their footwear in the car, he pointed to the sign that said, "Take off your shoes HERE!"

In a compilation that has three sections, the middle section deals with Hindutva, the Modi government, and other related issues, and it becomes clear where Capt. Gopinath stands—though he had once signed up and joined the Bharatiya Janta Party (BJP), hosting Atal Behari Vajpayee at a political rally in Hassan. His recounting of the syncretic traditions of Hindustani music sets up a counterpoint to the growing atmosphere of intolerance in the name of Hindu assertion.

In discussing the short-lived laws to reform agricultural marketing, Capt. Gopinath gets to the nub of the issue with the wisdom of someone who has tried his hand at farming and experienced its vagaries. Complex problems do not have instant magical solutions, reform of public procurement should not end up creating private cartels, and state governments should be involved. He closes the piece by quoting Tagore, 'the clumsiness of power spoils the key and uses the pickaxe.'

These references to select pieces should give the reader a flavour of what the book offers. There is variety aplenty: vignettes that offer thoughtful insights, commentary on passing events, pithy quotes, and flowing throughout the pages, a concern about the future the country is headed towards while being aware of the mistakes of the past. Capt. Gopinath is more than the sum of his parts: aviation pioneer, army officer, entrepreneur, political candidate, farmer, etc.; he is a concerned citizen.

T.N. Ninan
April 2022

# Author's Note

Our India, to each of us in our hearts and inner eyes, conjures a kaleidoscopic melange of images; memories from an immemorial past steeped in mythology and stories from epics; a people that came up with the Upanishads, profound philosophical treatises, a quest for the ultimate meaning of this universe; and an ancient civilisation that spawned and nurtured other great religions, embraced waves and waves of immigrants, a country that gave birth to great warrior kings like Chandragupta Maurya, whose empire stretched from the North-East to the North-West frontier province of the land well into present-day Afghanistan and till borders of Tamil Nadu in the South two thousand years ago. A civilisation that goes back 5000 years that absorbed hordes of invaders along with their ideas, their art, music and culture, ever changing, ever new but ever the same, a people who had a myriad gods but had the catholicity to appropriate other deities and make them its own from the Mahaveera, the Buddha to Guru Nanak; and took into its folds great Muslim Sufi saints like Mionuddin Chishti, bhakti poets like Kabir; a land that gave birth to the pacifist Emperor Ashoka, and to Akbar the Great, a formidable General and administrator, patron of arts and culture who brought together holy men of many faiths; Shankaracharya the most renowned propounder of Advaitha

Vedanta the linchpin of Hindu philosophy and Mahatma Gandhi the apostle of peace; great artists like saint Thyagaraja, Bismillah Khan and Bhimsen Joshi; to mesmerising temples like Madurai Meenakshi and mausoleums like the Taj Mahal; great forests, beaches and holy rivers like Ganges and Brahmaputra and to the majestic Himalayas, a land and its people that reveres living beings and sees God manifest in all animate and inanimate forms, such a land is truly unique and special. The foregoing names are a small number among a phalanx of sages and luminaries from millennia.

Our India, today, is in a tumultuous flux and at a crossroads. There is tremendous progress, large wealth creation, and millions lifted out of adversity. We are inheritors of a great heritage, a rich civilisational past but at present, we are also struggling with immense poverty, ignorance, disparity, inequality, social unrest, and strained communal harmony. Its rising intolerance amongst its various ethnic, caste and religious groups sooner or later is resisted and overcome by charitable forces that spring up from its fount of civilisational wellsprings and shared kinships. Its teeming diversity and seemingly disparate character is yet bound by an inextricable mystic bond unique to this land. Its multiplicity of ideas, plurality of faiths and philosophies are, on the contrary, a blessing. It has saved the nation from 'intellectual incest'. The sheer entrepreneurial energy, dynamism, and stoicism in the face of adversity of the masses warms one's heart, lifts one's spirits, and increases faith in the future of the nation which has survived and thrived for over five thousand years.

These opinion pieces are on a variety of topics: enterprise, the economy, government, politics, societal issues, and random, roving reflections - they were written over the last three years in varied publications, print, and online media platforms, such as the *Times of India, Economic Times, Deccan Herald, The Wire, The Print, Money Control*, and others. Some were commissioned by the editors, and others were spurred by the events that we witnessed in the country, at our borders and overseas.

They are not pedantic sermons. There is no pretence of scholarship here, nor domain depth. These impressions, seen together in one's mind's eye, may resemble a vast canvas on which a bewildered child has splashed colours, more akin to a palette than a painting. All the essays or vignettes, if I may be bold and risk sounding pretentious, are stories in the style of that incomparable master RK Narayan, the genial genius, woven with anecdotes from my personal experiences or seen through the prism of my acquaintance with humble vendors, a small family-owned bakery, an Udupi hotel, dhaba owners, migrant workers, farmers who are the real backbone of our economy, corporate leaders and idealistic entrepreneurs, politicians and ministers, but also foot soldiers and generals, great classical singers, writers, and many intrepid journalists and Godmen of all hues with whom I had deep-personal interactions.

Whether it is a story on love jihad, the dull topic of GST, the Chinese intrusions in the Galwan Valley of Ladakh, or the exodus of migrants; a pandemic death or the farmers' protest; encounters with politicians or artists or entrepreneurs, they are all tinged with a personal touch. In a way, they are subjective, even as I have tried to be objective.

A daring life in the Army and the terrible war with Pakistan in 1971, farming a barren land after becoming displaced due to the rising waters of a nearby dam, dabbling in a dozen startups, setting up an airline, flirting with politics, and contesting elections for a mainstream party, successes and failures, rising and falling and learning to dust oneself up to rise again by drawing strength from an inexplicable and inextinguishable optimism, encourage me to wake up every day with enthusiasm and not fall into a pit of despair or cynicism.

Losing one's loved ones in a war, or through a senseless wave of communal violence or a pandemic; or uprooting a business and livelihood when caught in the vortex of the inexorable march of events and the crossfire of brutal politics can be devastating and can crush the heart of the bravest individual. Yet we must pick up the loose ends and rise and march on stoically. As the great Ralph Waldo Emerson said, 'Skepticism is slow suicide.'

We must have the generosity of heart and spirit to admire people who are fighting hard and continually to make this a better world, do what we can to lessen evil and find joy in music and art and learn to forgive and forget through friendship, love and nature.

A poor farmer, despite floods and drought, and loss of his crops to the vagaries of nature, rises each morning with the sun, and shoulders to the plough, with his wife in tow, tills the land till dusk and sows the seeds, never questioning if the sun will shine the next morning and never doubting that rain will sprout the seeds.

He has faith and hope, that tomorrow will be a better day, the good earth will smile with her blossoms and ripen with harvests. Who can cease to be inspired by him and his steadfast companion?

*Faith is the bird that feels the light when the dawn is still dark.*
– Rabindranath Tagore

Captain G.R. Gopinath
Bengaluru
28 April 2022

PS – There may be a few repetitions of thoughts and quotations in some articles written over the years. The more things change, the more they are the same. I beg the reader's indulgence.

# ENTERPRISE

# The Cook, The Colonel and The Pandemic

Dinesh had two traits that stood out – an iron will and discipline. At five every evening, on the dot, come rain or sunshine, he would jump into his track pants and bolt from the house for his karate classes. He would return home by seven in the evening, drenched in sweat, shower in a jiffy and with a glowing smile be ready to cook the evening meal. On occasion, he would return beaten black and blue but plunge into his chores joyfully and narrate tales of his exploits during dinner – of how he was thrashed by a much bigger fighter.

Then one day, after five or six years, he came to us to say he had earned his karate black belt and wished to venture out on his own and set up a martial arts school. I was thrilled, though also sad that he was leaving us.

Years passed. Dinesh kept in touch. His start-up expanded to two locations. He had tiny tots, youngsters from schools and colleges and professionals from the Tatas and Toyota and others training under him. He had married a young girl from Nepal. With the great reversal of his social status and financial standing, he beamed with pride.

And last month, suddenly, he came home to see me. The light in his eyes was dim, the lustre on his face had disappeared, the spring in his step was absent. The pandemic had taken its toll. His martial arts school was shut. He was unschooled but had braved on by taking online classes. The number of students had shrunk. His income had plummeted. He had bank debts and private loans to discharge. Added to it, he had to pay monthly rents for the karate school and his house and had now a family to care for. He had three assistants whom he had to let go. He was now staring at an uncertain future. The coronavirus had upended his business and life.

Col. Vaidyanathan (Vaidy) had retired after twenty years of service as an army engineer. A common friend directed him to me. He always had this fire in the belly to become an entrepreneur. So, he decided to set up a gourmet restaurant in Bangalore. The Colonel loved authentic rural Punjabi cuisine. He recruited two Sikh chefs from Amritsar who specialized in kulchas and brought them to Bangalore and launched the restaurant Kulcha di Hatti in an upscale locality. The venture took off to roaring success. Then COVID-19 happened and the March 2020 national lockdown. His restaurant ground to a halt. He held on and kept his chefs and staff on payroll. He had trained them with army rigour. After three months, there were relaxations. On a wing and a prayer, he re-opened the restaurant. But the virus hovered about. The business never picked up. His losses and debts mounted. His retirement savings evaporated. Unable to sustain, he shut shop. It was gut-wrenching. He retrenched his staff of fifteen. The ground beneath him suddenly collapsed. He is undaunted, picking up the pieces, and now looking at new opportunities to start over again.

The real engine that keeps the Indian economy running is made up of the millions of small entrepreneurs in a myriad of enterprises. The majority of jobs are generated by tiny corner groceries, Udupi hotels, bakeries and dhabas, fruit and vegetable vendors, restaurants, spas and salons, lodges and home-stays and countless self-employed drivers, mechanics, weavers, handicrafts artisans, pavement and pushcart sellers, etc. And, of course, in addition, there are lakhs of small- and medium-sized producers of goods and services, the very breath of economic activity.

The hard numbers tell the story. Government (states and Centre put together) and corporate employees add up to some 50 million people. Public sector enterprises, including the railways and the armed forces, together account for another 5 million jobs. That means, out of an employable 750 million of our 1.3 billion population, just about 55 million are in the organized sector. About 350 million (farmers and rural labour) are employed in agriculture activities. That leaves the rest, nearly 350 million (which includes urban labour) – nearly 50 per cent of the employable population – engaged in various small occupations, enterprises and services.

These unknown entrepreneurs are fired more by their imagination and entrepreneurial drive than seed capital. They overcome obstacles at every step with stoic courage and somehow survive the 'inspector raj' that preys on them. They create new and different markets, jobs and wealth where none existed before.

The solutions to bail them out are not easy. Authentic and reliable data on these self-employed are hard to come by. But the government must find ways to come to their aid.

The slightly larger small- and medium-sized enterprises (SMEs), about whom data is available, are in dire straits. A mandatory moratorium of two years on principle and interest payments, with waiver of penalties, on bank loans to all SMEs may be one way of giving them succour. The government can advance matching amounts as loans to banks for two years to shore up their liquidity. Along with it, a moratorium on the goods and services tax (GST) without penalties for two years from March 2020 can also be offered. These measures could, to an extent, help them pay salaries and avoid retrenchment of staff. The present directive by the government instructing banks to restructure loans of the SMEs is not achieving the desired objectives. Banks are risk-averse, especially with the self-employed and SMEs.

If the government protects small entrepreneurs and their enterprises, they will, in turn, protect jobs and create new ones. Prime Minister Modi must enable them to live to fight another day because once slain, they can never rise to fight again.

*Deccan Herald*, July 2021

# I Want to Own a Bank. Don't Let Me!

First, a confession is in order. Would I want to own a bank and have a key to the bank treasury to start a new airline? You bet! Can I promise that I won't dip my hands into the till when my airline runs out of cash? Don't you doubt it. And will I recuse myself where needed and follow corporate governance? Of course. Anything for the keys to the bank safe. If you ask a fox that is in charge of the henhouse to promise not to eat the chicks if he is hungry, what would he say? My promise would be as sacrosanct as his. You don't give the keys of a henhouse to a fox. Not even to a virtuous fox. Period.

But the Reserve Bank of India (RBI), the last guardian of India's financial and banking system, wants to do just that. That the RBI constituted an Internal Working Group to determine if large corporate houses can be given licence to promote banks and recommended that they be allowed to operate banks, all without inviting a larger public debate, is unconscionable. Banking regulations for licensing have not been diluted in the last fifty years to allow business barons to promote a bank. Whenever these requests came up, they were always frowned upon. That the RBI has recommended it even after its own Internal Working Group 'found out from its set of experts that barring one, all of them were of the opinion that large corporate/industrial houses should not be allowed to promote a bank' is baffling.

## Not a welcome move

In a joint paper posted on 23 November 2020, former RBI Governor Raghuram Rajan and former RBI Deputy Governor Viral Acharya termed the recommendations allowing corporates into banking a 'bombshell' and said this proposal is 'best left on the shelf'. Referring to business houses owning an in-house bank that may lead to self-lending, they said, 'The history of such connected lending is invariably disastrous – how can the bank make good loans when it is owned by the borrower? Even an independent committed regulator, with all the information in the world, finds it difficult to be in every nook and corner of the financial system to stop poor lending. Information on loan performance is rarely timely or accurate. Yes Bank managed to conceal its weak exposures for considerable periods.'

Indeed, anything coming from Mr Rajan or Mr Acharya may be seen as being partisan or motivated by the present dispensation. But other experts have also not welcomed this move. Professor T.T. Ram Mohan wrote in this newspaper, 'If the record of over-leveraging in the corporate world in recent years is anything to go by, the entry of corporate houses into banking is a road to perdition.' Hemindra Hazari, a well-known Securities and Exchange Board of India (SEBI) research analyst, wrote in an article titled 'RBI's working group recommends foxes be put in charge of chicken coops': 'Even under the existing financial regime, the RBI was unable to detect at an early stage the connected lending which felled large regulated financial entities like IL&FS, Yes Bank (Rana Kapoor and his entities held 10.6% as on end September 2018), Punjab and Maharashtra Co-operative Bank and DHFL (promoter holding 39%). Will it be able to effectively regulate and monitor large, complex industrial houses which are well versed in disguising financial transactions through a vast web of opaque domestic and foreign-based entities?' In a blistering critique in Bloomberg titled 'India's banking rules need to close door to tycoon cronyism', renowned analyst Andy Mukherjee wrote: 'From telecommunications to transportation, India's business landscape is already starting to resemble a Monopoly board.' He recommended less risky options of asking corporates who promote banks to pare down their shareholding to 15 per cent over the long term and penalties for misdemeanours and connected lending violations by bringing down their voting rights to 5 per cent.

The RBI is overlooking time-tested principles and limits of disallowing mega business houses from promoting and owning banks. It is saying this can be done by making necessary amendments to the Banking Regulation Act of 1949 to deal with connected lending and linkages between banks and non-financial group entities and strengthening the supervisory mechanism for conglomerates. This is in stark departure from its long-held opinion on the subject since 1969, when banks were nationalized. History is replete with evidence of business barons who were good when they started out, only to eventually morph into robber barons who not only enriched themselves owing to their enormous wealth and nexus with politicians in power but also crushed competition. It will be naive to believe that a bank owned by a corporate house will permit lending to its competitors. Mr Mukherjee ended his article eloquently, saying, 'To roll out red carpet to wannabe JP Morgans would be an abdication of the RBI's financial stability and mandate.'

## The way forward

Public sector banks may be inefficient and indifferent and under the influence of the party in power, but private sector banks that are owned by oligarchs and business tycoons in cahoots with politicians will be rapacious monsters. The way forward should be to privatize public sector banks by allowing wide and diversified holding of stock by the general public. If the government exits banking ownership, that would lead to professional management and broader distribution of wealth. The banks would come under both SEBI and stringent RBI guidelines.

Many a time when my company could not manage to restructure its loan and ended up in Debts Recovery Tribunals, how I wished I owned a bank! How can we expect virtue from modern-day business maharajas when in the Mahabharata, even King Yudhishthira gambled away his wife, family and kingdom?

*The Hindu*, December 2020

# Man Cannot Live by the Internet Alone

The just-concluded initial public offering (IPO) of Zomato, which has successfully raised about ₹9,000 crore at an astronomical valuation of ₹66,000 crore, makes one believe that money does grow on trees.

More than 150 years ago, Leo Tolstoy, one of the greatest novelists and thinkers of the world, writing in his book *What Then Must We Do*, wondered: 'If everything of value and substance is produced in the rural areas, why then are the villages mired in poverty and cities awash in wealth?' That question continues to befuddle us.

## The old conundrum

All these thoughts brought back memories of my own life from the 1980s. In those days, I was struggling as a farmer to make ends meet. I toiled all day, living out of a second-hand army tent in a remote part of rural Karnataka. One day, after harvesting the banana crop and loading it onto my tractor well before dawn, I drove it to the weekly farmers' market in Hassan, the district headquarters. As I approached the main road leading to the market, my tractor stopped behind a massive row of trucks and vehicles, hundreds of them, all belonging to other farmers. Walking up a kilometre, I came across thousands of agitated farmers. They had unloaded their fresh green chillies and tomatoes onto the road, and the black tarmac had turned red and green. The heady, pungent fumes from the crushed chillies made it impossible to breathe. Discovering that the prices had crashed, the farmers were up in arms as they were not even able to recover the transportation costs. So, they had blocked the roads. Around noon, finally extricating myself from the melee, unable to sell my produce and crestfallen, I ferried the bananas back to my farm and fed them to my cattle.

Zomato's IPO event also reminded me of those days when banks repeatedly turned down my request for an agriculture loan of ₹1 lakh but two decades later, a bank sanctioned an eye-popping amount of ₹500 crore on a silver platter to my low-cost airline as the airline was publicly listed and a highly valued stock. The value lay in the mind's eye of the beholder, who, unbeknownst to me, was in thrall to mythic bears and bulls who swayed the bourses.

All these strange phenomena of the modern economy hark back to the old conundrum: how is it that those farmers who own land, toil and till, produce real stuff that we eat and drink and touch and feel, produce things that keep us fed and warm – grains, fruits, vegetables, meat, cotton, wool, silk and so on – live in destitution whereas the merchant who peddles them or the broker who speculates is rich? The multinational behemoths that retail groceries and other products (Kraft Heinz, Cargill, Tyson Foods, Danone, Nestle, Unilever, Walmart, Reliance) and those that build solid steel plants, automobiles, buildings, bridges, ships, railways and hotel chains may, in turn, wonder why they do all the heavy lifting but are overshadowed in their stock market valuation by Amazon, Microsoft, Tata Consultancy Services (TCS) and Infosys. And now, the new kids on the block – Byju's, Zomato and Paytm – are more valuable than those that have been working for decades. The Manipal Group, for instance, runs scores of medical and engineering colleges and hospitals. It owns hundreds of acres of prime land across cities in India and even overseas. It has massive education complexes and impressive laboratories, medical diagnostics equipment and surgical operation theatres. Despite thousands of crores of investments and hundreds of professors and doctors and nurses, it is valued at a fraction of Byju's.

Similarly, the Taj Hotels, Oberoi Hotels and other five-star hotels own the most expensive real estate. They have luxurious rooms and suites, gourmet restaurants, spas and salons and swimming pools fit for maharajahs. But they are valued at less than a fraction of Zomato. And Zomato, which produces nothing and only purveys the food made by innumerable restaurants across the country, has almost twice the valuation of Jubilant FoodWorks, which owns Domino's Pizza. While others make profits, Zomato and the new unicorns all bleed cash but have dizzying valuations.

I met Neeraj Gupta of Meru Cabs, who was the first entrepreneur to launch nationwide GPS-linked radio taxis in India. He revolutionized urban mobility a few years ago. He owned more than 3,000 cars then. His company now has a fleet of 9,000 cars. But Uber and Ola, which manage a few lakh taxis across the metros of India, have upended his business model. These are asset-light companies that only manage the taxis enlisted on their Internet platform. They meet the needs of customers with optimal, effective and timely use of available resources but have heady market caps. I am not discrediting these Internet companies. These are indeed brilliant concepts.

## A good life

Information and data are said to be the new fuel of the modern economy. The Internet makes the world go round and round and the stock valuations of new-age companies can orbit you into space.

But there is limited space in that stratosphere. This world, and life on it, cannot be circumscribed in a make-believe cloud. You can't eat information and everyone cannot live in the Internet bubble. We need food, clothing, water, housing, transportation, electricity and hospitals, and also flowers, poetry and art. We need education in schools and university campuses where there are teachers in flesh and blood and where breezy, invigorating dialogue, debate, bonhomie, music and laughter reign. We need restaurants and travel, and beaches with sun, sand and wine and kisses. We need stout, hearty men and women who work with their hands to provide for the world. All that makes for a good life.

That may not make you a billionaire, which the sterile world of the Internet economy can make you, but don't be disheartened or discouraged. That real world rooted in the earth and soil I speak of can create wealth too. It can give abundant joy and meaning if you do your job with passion and commitment.

Then my thoughts turned to my wife's twenty-five-year-old Iyengar Bakery tucked away in Malleswaram, Bangalore. It is a landmark eatery, which is loved and patronized by the local residents. It is part of the cultural landscape. Her wealth has not soared like the stocks of Internet companies. But she is happy and content and loves making breads and buns every day. And she is the master of her own universe.

There are countless such people across India in myriad fields – farmers, teachers, doctors, writers, journalists, masons, carpenters, blacksmiths, mechanics, artists, artisans, grocers and vendors – who serve their communities and provide jobs, livelihoods and security. They make this a wonderful world. Man cannot live by the Internet alone.

*The Hindu*, July 2021

# Finding a Match for the Maharaja: Reminiscences from a Painful Stake Sale and Lessons for Air India

It was heart-wrenching. The year was 2007, and Kingfisher Airlines had taken over the beloved airline I had founded along with my former army-aviation colleagues just four years ago.

We wept.

At the time, I remember some journalists asking me how I felt. And I told them that it was like marrying off my daughter. Now, Air India as a brand may not be identified by most Indians as 'The National Carrier' having been over shadowed by other domestic carriers.

There's a fond nostalgia associated with the airline, and it evokes a vague feeling of loss whenever the topic of Air India's sale crops up. Indeed, there is resistance against privatizing the airline, but it's all just romantic mush, and sentiment must not override commercial decisions when public money is involved.

After all, Air India is not India.

## When silver turns into lead

Originally, it was a great private airline set up by J.R.D. Tata and was imprudently nationalized when Jawaharlal Nehru was the Prime Minister, and now it has been run to the ground. The airline's losses are being funded by the Indian taxpayers, its real owners. IndiGo, SpiceJet, GoAir and other airlines are as much Indian as Air India. All this talk of Air India airlifting stranded passengers or immigrants from foreign countries to justify it continuing as the national carrier under government control is baloney.

True, it has done a commendable job whenever pressed into service. IndiGo, Vistara or SpiceJet would have done the same had they been entrusted with the task. British Airways, Lufthansa and Air France, which were all once government-owned national carriers, besides American Airlines and many other airlines, have been carrying out similar rescue missions for their respective countries.

Successive governments at the centre have postponed the sale of the airline, citing that it was 'family silver'. They chose to overlook that the silver was fast turning into lead. The real reasons for holding on to Air India may not be that lofty. It is not run like a commercial airline but is treated like a 'joint-family airline' for bureaucrats who don't want to let go of it. But over the years, it has become sloppy, with ministers giving jobs at the airline to people from their respective constituencies.

I once confronted Sharad Yadav, who was then the aviation minister, after he was criticized for indiscriminate recruitment of people in Air India's Class IV category. With a mischievous twinkle in his eyes, Yadav said, 'Gopi Chand ji, do you know that 10 per cent of the employees – high-end management, pilots, engineers and others – pocket 90 per cent of the total salary at Air India? So, adding another three thousand employees or more in the lowest salary bracket won't make any difference to the overall kitty.'

I was astounded at his astute analysis of the expenditure pie chart. He was trying to be a well-meaning socialist, but with no accountability. As far as he was concerned, Air India was just another government department.

The above factors may explain the flip-flops and the ham-handed way in which the Air India sale has been steered all these years, and why there are no suitors yet for the state-run airline.

In this context, aviation minister Hardeep Singh Puri's recent admission in Parliament – that 'with ₹60,000 crore debt, the choice is not between privatization and non-privatization … but between privatization and closing down' – is a breath of fresh air. It is praiseworthy of the minister to have recognized the reality.

As an entrepreneur, I can relate to the longing to hold on to one's own venture. Many founders of companies suffer from this emotional blind spot, and it can be fatal for a private company. Delay, prevarication and a lack of sense of timing and grasp of the nature of the crisis, apart from dispassionate and objective assessment of the situation, can wreck a business and put all its stakeholders at risk. Any hesitation in grabbing an opportunity to bring in an external investor can be the difference between life and death.

A promoter must recognize that howsoever gut-wrenching it may be to part with the company they have founded, they owe it to the shareholders and employees and should therefore rise above temptations and do the right thing.

## A dream takes wings

The collapse of Jet Airways and the recent statement by Puri take me back to the old days when I had to take a call to bring in fresh investors into Air Deccan. That meant ceding control of the airline I had so lovingly and assiduously built and handing it over on a platter to an outsider.

I was obsessed to the point of madness with Air Deccan, which I had started with ₹5 crore of borrowed capital from an investor who believed in me and my dream by facilitating some additional bank guarantees. We had started our operations with five used regional ATR planes.

The ultra-low-cost no-frills model clicked, and we started expanding at breakneck speed. We deployed forty-eight aircraft (twenty-three ATRs and twenty-five Airbus) in forty-eight months. We overtook Indian Airlines (now Air India) in market share in the third year and glazed past Jet Airways' domestic market share at 24.5 per cent (in terms of passenger market share and not revenue) in the fourth year of operations. We were the number one in network, touching seventy airports – twenty-five of them regional towns that were connected for the first time. Belgaum, Hubballi, Bellary, Rajahmundry, Tuticorin, Vijayawada, Jabalpur, Gwalior, Kolhapur, Sholapur, Jamshedpur, Kullu, Shimla, Dharamshala, Pathankot, Dehradun … we connected them all and many more small towns, penetrating deep into the bowels of the country.

Along with fares starting at ₹1, there was an implosion in demand, and a tectonic consumer shift on a societal scale was clearly evident. It was no magic. The feat was achieved through constant innovation and the courage and commitment of my team.

The airline needed cash for expansion, but we did not wait for the consolidation of our balance sheet. Instead, we opted for fresh equity from the private sector and from the public through stock listing, which diluted the promoters' stake, including mine, to fund the expansion.

I wanted to dominate the market and raise more equity as the airline expanded to prevent predatory pricing from Jet Airways.

## Turbulence begins

And then, lightning struck. Five more airlines entered the business, encouraged by the success of Air Deccan. Meanwhile, crude oil prices shot above $130 per barrel and were on a boil. There was an acute shortage of pilots and engineers. New airlines started poaching talent from each other, and flights had to be often grounded as pilots and engineers didn't show up in the morning. Salaries of captains went through the roof – from ₹1.5 lakh when we started operations to ₹5 lakh within three years. There were no parking slots at the airports.

The concept of selling air tickets through Internet-reservation systems, though pioneered by Air Deccan, was sabotaged by a rival carrier. Airlines started heavy discounting and undercutting prices to fill planes. All airlines started haemorrhaging cash.

My investors had deep pockets, but they panicked. We were the largest airline by market share and network with hardly any debt and had placed orders for sixty Airbus and thirty ATRs with the best pricing contracts. Remember, 'Vision is the art of seeing the invisible.'

But unfortunately, my private equity partners were not seeing what I was seeing and weren't ready to open their purse strings and increase their own equity. I was looking at the long term, but they wanted to cash out and make a quick windfall. The market cap of Air Deccan was inching towards a billion dollars by the end of the fourth year of starting operations. But I was losing money and realized that I would soon run out of cash to meet the current liabilities such as salaries, fuel, and payments to vendors and suppliers.

Still, Air Deccan was making waves. The brand was hot, and investment bankers were on the prowl to take us over. Unbeknown to me, the private equity partners had even unofficially floated the word around that they were looking to exit.

I was tempted to say 'no' to my partners and ride out the storm. Running an airline can be intoxicating with all its associated power, glamour and pure adrenaline rush. With 1,000 pilots and engineers, 800 air hostesses and more joining every day, you are on a perennial 'high'.

Like a man possessed, I was on a mission to make every Indian fly – a vision that cannot be realized in one's lifetime. My partners sensed this and tried to reason with me, pointing out that my ego was coming in the way and was harming their interests. They asked me what if I couldn't pull it off and the airline went belly up. There was no easy way out – either I had to buy them out or allow new investors to purchase their stake.

## A change of mind

I could have dug in my heels and not agreed to dilute my stake to raise more equity. It would have only created a crisis. I knew that a conflict with partners would be the beginning of the end for the airline. The wise words of my first chartered accountant, Balakrishna Achar, rang aloud inside me.

Nearly twenty-five years ago, when I first chose to be an entrepreneur after leaving the Indian Army and had set up a Royal Enfield motorcycle dealership in Hassan in Karnataka, he had told me, 'Choose your partners well.' It is easier to divorce your wife than your business partners.

I didn't sleep all night. By morning, I knew that I should not lose even a moment in bringing onboard a new investor and must do everything to help my existing partners exit with good returns. The word got around, and investment bankers and some corporate houses started calling me. And with the buzz entering the media, the company's stock price started going up. Potential investors get put off when the stock price climbs too high.

It was amidst all this that I got a call from Anil Ambani's office.

'Captain, I heard you're keen on raising more equity, and I'm keen to invest,' Ambani said.

I was taken by surprise and told him I would get back. Then, I got a call from a minister who said I should not let my ego come in the way. He added that my name would always be etched in the history of Indian aviation and I must strike a good deal for investors as it would also turn out to be a big boost for Air Deccan's growth. I knew him well, and he was not arm-twisting me.

'I'm not interfering in the details. Please do the deal if you get the right valuation for Air Deccan,' he said.

Ambani, a master in acquisitions and hostile takeovers, was a formidable name, and I was apprehensive. I was a small-town guy – an entrepreneur who had never swum in the high seas of commerce where sharks lurk.

So, I immediately called K.V. Kamath, the then chairman of ICICI Bank. I had heard that the Ambani family held him in high esteem and hence asked Kamath if he could act as a goodwill ambassador to instil confidence on both sides so that a deal could be finalized swiftly.

I flew to Mumbai and was taken from the Santacruz Airport to Ambani's sprawling corporate office in Navi Mumbai in his helicopter. He was bubbling with energy and spoke nonstop for four hours.

He was full of ideas but mostly referred to them in anecdotes with frequent reminiscences of his father, the great Dhirubhai Ambani. Those four hours gave me a peep into the mind of India's original entrepreneur. After that, he treated me to the best Gujarati feast of my life. He served the dishes himself. Needless to say, I was floored.

The next meeting was in Kamath's office. The shrewd and soft-spoken banker was gracious and created the ideal atmosphere for discussions. By evening, the deal was done, and a detailed term sheet was signed by both of us, offering a 51 per cent stake to Ambani's Reliance Anil Dhirubhai Ambani Group (ADAG) at an agreed premium above the share price. The agreed equity investment was to be made within a fortnight and was subject to the approval of the Air Deccan board.

## When hope comes crashing

When I returned to Bangalore, my investors were ecstatic. The media had got a whiff of the deal, and *The Economic Times* ran a story titled 'ADA likely to board Air Deccan flight'. The stock zoomed.

Soon after the *ET* report, I got a call from Vijay Mallya. He wanted to meet me.

By then, we were at each other's throats, and I was very upset with him because he had been poaching my pilots. On an earlier occasion, when he had publicly asked me to allow him to invest, I had declined, saying that 'Vijay is from Mars, and I'm from Venus'. Ever since, I had been avoiding his calls.

Then a Karnataka minister called me and convinced me to at least answer his call and listen to what he had to say. I felt it was prudent to avoid the meeting with Mallya since the term sheet with Ambani was already in place.

Soon, Ambani called me and said it would be a good idea to meet the aviation minister and shake hands in his presence and inform him about the deal. I thought it might not be the right thing to do as we were a listed entity. But Ambani was of the view that we should inform the minister in a private meeting as a matter of courtesy. I agreed, and both of us met the minister in Delhi.

But on the due date mentioned on the term sheet, there was no news from Ambani or his office. Naturally, I was anxious. Then I got a call from ADAG's Chief Financial Officer Amitabh Jhunjhunwala.

'We are also negotiating to acquire SpiceJet. So, we thought we must announce the deal together. It will make a big splash. Besides, it will be a huge consolidation, and the eventual merger will make us very strong. So, we will complete the deal in fifteen days from today,' he told me.

I was upset, and hence curt. 'Fine, then the deal is off. If I'm still unmarried by then, you can tie the knot,' I said before hanging up.

I immediately called up Bhulo Kansagra, one of the lead promoters of SpiceJet, which was still taking baby steps at the time and was desperate for funds. Meanwhile, another SpiceJet promoter, Ajay Singh, confirmed the development.

'Yes, Anil Ambani is in touch [with SpiceJet] and dialogue is in progress. Are you fine with the eventual acquisition and merger of both Spice and Air Deccan?' he quizzed. I said it would be good in the long term.

Kansagra called me back later and said that the Tatas already had a 7 per cent stake in SpiceJet and asked if I was okay for a merger with SpiceJet, with Tata acquiring a majority stake in both airlines instead of a deal with Ambani. That sounded good. Kansagra, who was based in London, said he would check with Ratan Tata and fly down immediately.

## 'Cheers' to the deal

In the meantime, Mallya had been calling me almost every day but I was still evading. On the day the term sheet with Ambani expired and I told Jhunjhunwala that I wasn't bound by it any longer but my arms will be open if I'm still single when he had the money, a minister in the Karnataka government came home to see me.

He wanted to know the details of the agreement with Ambani and whether the deal was already done. I said the term sheet had expired that very day, and Ambani had requested fifteen more days, but I was in talks with other prospective investors. The minister then asked me if I would refuse it if Mallya were to make a better offer. 'He's a Kannadiga who is already in the airline business, and you know each other. Why don't you say hello to him once and listen to what he has to say,' the minister said, and dialled Mallya before I could respond.

'Gopi, I heard about the deal. Can you give me a chance?' Mallya asked.

'Vijay, we are from different planets. You discredit low-cost airlines. Your model is super-luxury; it is not scalable in a country like ours,' I tried to reason.

'Gopi, that's all rivalry talk. I know about low-cost. I am the largest seller of low-cost whisky in the world – Bagpiper. Even a low-cost man like you won't drink that. Let's do the deal.'

'You don't have the time, Vijay,' I shot back.

'How many days do I have to pay you?'

'Three days. Anil missed the legal deadline today and has requested for three or four more days, if not fifteen.'

Without hesitation, he said, 'Done. I'm in Monte Carlo now for the Formula One. [I] Will call you around ten tonight from my yacht after the race. I am hosting a dinner on the yacht. Whatever is the offer of Anil, I will better it. Don't do the deal with others. Bye.'

I was speechless. Meanwhile, the minister was beaming like a Cheshire cat, toasting a drink.

The phone rang at ten that night. Mallya, notorious for not adhering to schedule and known to keep people waiting, was intuitive enough to realize that it would be unwise to postpone this call.

'Gopi, I'm on the yacht. Guests are streaming in.'

I could hear peals of laughter and greetings and could imagine the swish, glamorous set of swashbuckling men and beautiful women sashaying in silk. I could even smell the heady melange of exotic perfumes and hear the music in the background.

'Can you note down all the points?' Mallya said, shaking me out of my thoughts. 'I will settle the guests and call you after two to three hours. We will close the broad terms of the deal in half-hour. Please, can you accommodate me?'

I was a bit upset, but it was no time to allow my personal emotions to derail the mission at hand.

'Sure, Vijay. Let's fix a time. You know I won't keep waiting for you.'

'Sure, Gopi. I will call you sharp at one, India time.'

The phone rang well past midnight. 'Gopi, Vijay here. Sorry for waking you up.'

Now, Mallya is not exactly the kind to apologize for being late. It gave me an inkling that he was desperate to do the deal and see Kingfisher Airlines fly abroad as the rules then mandated a minimum of five years' service to operate foreign flights. Air Deccan could enable that for Kingfisher as it had been operational for the required period. Further, since Air Deccan was listed, it would make it easier for Mallya to raise money from the market.

The conversation that followed went on like this (the figures are approximate).

'Vijay, get hold of a pen. Here we go,' I said. 'First, I want ₹160 per share. Second, I will be the chairman, and you can be the vice chairman. Third, we will have twelve directors, out of which I will appoint three, and you can pick three, while the six independent directors are to be jointly appointed. Four, a professional CEO will be appointed jointly by me and you to run Air Deccan and report to its board.'

Elaborating my terms, I told him that the above would translate into around ₹500 crore in investments in Air Deccan for a 26 per cent stake.

'You have to infuse ₹500 crore more via purchase of shares in the open offer. I want an advance from you in demand draft in favour of Air Deccan for ₹200 crore within three days, delivered at Deccan's office along with a binding term sheet. I will call a board meeting only after that and present the proposal to the board. The balance ₹300 crore should be invested within thirty days, or else the advance of ₹200 crore will be forfeited,' I added.

Here, it is pertinent to note that contrary to the general perception, I did not sell the airline to Mallya by transferring my shares or those of my other promoter-friend to collect ₹500 crore. I neither sold even one share to Mallya nor received a rupee for it. I was getting him to invest in Air Deccan so that I could continue to be involved with my airline.

'Yes, Gopi, done,' he replied. 'My president Ravi Nedungadi will contact you tomorrow to work out and close the term sheet. The demand draft will be delivered in Deccan's corporate office on Wednesday. I've got to run; the guests are waiting. Cheers.'

I could imagine him dissolving back into that happy world of fashionable women, and rich and gallant men of high society as his yacht of glitz and glamour swayed on the Mediterranean waves.

I wasn't sure if I was dreaming, for the deal was done in flat thirty minutes. It was probably faster than his Formula One cars.

I rubbed my eyes.

The next day, Kansagra called and said Ratan Tata was open to the idea of acquiring both the airlines, and he was taking the next flight to London, and I should be ready to fly to Mumbai for discussions. The Mallya ball was still in the air.

Nedungadi and his team of lawyers were sitting with my team to draft the term sheet. But a deal is not done until it is done. So, I kept my doors open to Kansagra for a possible deal with the Tatas. After all, I told myself that day, 'Who knows if Vijay would pull out at the last moment. For all I know, Anil may emerge again and seal the deal. Anything can happen.'

It was on Tuesday – a day before the demand draft and term sheet were signed with Kingfisher – that I received a call from Dayanidhi Maran, enquiring if Mallya was actually acquiring Air Deccan. I said we had reached an agreement and were expected to sign it the next day. Maran (who later went on to buy SpiceJet) said if the deal did not materialize, he would fly down next day as he was ready to invest and match the other offers. I told him I would be happy to contact him in the case of such an outcome.

And on the appointed day, the demand draft arrived, and the board approved the deal in a jiffy. Mallya invested and eventually took control of Air Deccan. What transpired after he came on board, how it all panned out, the roller-coaster ride of Kingfisher and Air Deccan with Mallya at the helm is a story for another day.

I called up Kansagra and explained to him as to why I could not take the risk of putting Mallya on hold in anticipation of the Tatas taking a call on acquiring both our airlines.

## Back to Air India

The foregoing story in such detail is necessary to put in proper context as to why purposive direction, speed and a kind of paranoia to close deals, especially when companies are bleeding and losing value every day, are paramount.

The absence of a sense of ownership at Air India, where losses don't pinch anyone personally but are still a big drain on the public exchequer, coupled with varied opinions, conflict of interests and the involvement of multiple forces, end up foiling the attempts of a few well-meaning individuals in the government to sell the national carrier.

Therefore, Hardeep Singh Puri's initiative to take charge and steer the auction brings cheer. As he rightly observed, 'Closing cannot be an option. A going concern fetches money, but a grounded airline goes for scrap.'

But to pull off a successful auction, Puri must move with a sense of urgency and purpose to find a groom for an ageing bride whose alluring charm has almost faded. That will be his crowning glory. By now, it must have dawned on him that if you do the same things over and over you reap the same results – and there will still be no suitors for Air India.

*The Economic Times*, September 2020

# The Triumphs and Tragedy of Café Coffee Day's Siddhartha

When you write an obituary of a fellow entrepreneur whom you admire, who has committed suicide by jumping off a bridge, a chilling thought lurks inside: 'It could have been me floating in the river.' Life is not easy. Life is also unfair, as John F. Kennedy said.

Some overwhelming circumstance, a crushing blow, a seemingly impossible situation, a cruel word from a near and dear relative or friend to whom one may reach out in a trying situation – any of this could push anyone, even the strongest, over the edge. All entrepreneurs face it. Every human being goes through periods of doubt and despair. The spirit and flesh both give up. We somehow hold on, summon the courage to take counsel and rise again.

Still, one feeling haunts. Oh, if only Siddhartha had shared his thoughts, his travails and trepidations with a friend or associate, this unspeakable tragedy wouldn't have happened. If he had somehow held on and faced the challenge, he would surely have overcome his difficulties once again, as he had done countless times earlier. If only he had not taken that fatal jump, he would have found a way out of the impasse.

Other images and memories crowd the mind. My first meeting with Siddhartha in the mid-1990s is still vivid. He had made his maiden equity investment in the IT company Mindtree and reached out to me for a helicopter charter to ferry the CEO of the Bank of America to his tech park in the suburbs of Bangalore, where the inaugural function was held. He was tall, slim of build, sharp and unassuming, with a pleasing demeanour. I instantly took a liking to him.

I instinctively admired him for his entrepreneurial instincts. He was not a technocrat, nor did he possess an MBA from IIM or other Ivy Leagues like Harvard; he was a local graduate who had dared to become a venture capitalist when venture capitalists didn't exist in India. Not only was he a venture capitalist but also an entrepreneur himself.

Over the next two and a half decades, our paths as entrepreneurs, being in the same city and hailing from the same districts, often crossed. He never failed to accept invitations to social functions but didn't stay longer than half an hour. He was shy, a teetotaller who held a glass of wine out of courtesy. He never hung around and quietly left without pomp or fuss.

But what really captivated me about him over the years as I watched him were his entrepreneurial instincts, uncanny grasp of business and shrewd understanding of politics and its dangerous undercurrents. He possessed a native management acumen to structure an organization and surround himself with capable people. He exuded indefatigable energy and, above all, a grand vision with a tenacity rarely seen to pursue the goal that he had set for himself.

## The Air Deccan partnership

He was quick to grasp a proposal or business idea and could go straight to where the matter hinged. One small example from my dealings with him will suffice. When I started the low-cost airline Air Deccan, I wished to sell everything on board, including water, to the passengers on the flight, unlike the practice then of supplying lunch, dinner or snacks free of charge, procuring from Taj or Oberoi five-star inflight catering, the only facility available until then.

Café Coffee Day by then probably had about sixty outlets, fast expanding and present in several of the major and regional cities where Air Deccan flew. My proposal was simple. I was offering a shopping mall to Siddhartha's Café Coffee Day – the Airbus – without rent, electricity or water tariffs or the octroi and sundry cesses, and with a fully furnished interior with zero capital investment, with my air hostesses as sales girls and captive customers for an hour or two to whom he could sell snacks and coffee. I said all losses, wastage and profits were his and demanded to offer Air Deccan a 30 per cent commission.

Siddhartha's face lit up. He saw in a flash that the offer had great brand value for his expansion. In his mind's eye, there must have rolled visions of hundreds of his Coffee Day outlets mushrooming across the country, giving a boost to his brand through the flying outlets crisscrossing the country. He sealed the deal in less than an hour.

But it is his unmatched feat of creating a network of 1,750 outlets in every nook and corner of the country that takes your breath away. The first seven to eight years, he had just a handful of Coffee Day shops in Bangalore, having started the first one on the famous Brigade Road. He called them internet cafes to attract the new millennials. Once he studied, thought through and fine-tuned the business model, he unleashed all his pent-up ideas and expanded with breakneck speed.

## Extraordinary feats

Creating such a vast network that is not a franchise model but an ownership model involves the acquisition of real estate, infrastructure, furnishings and branding, recruitment of manpower, IT infrastructure, brand communication, among others. The sheer logistics and complexity of supply chain in a food industry that's perishable is a Himalayan task. Ordinary mortals can't accomplish such deeds.

The thought again returns to torment. Why did an extraordinary individual who had already faced overwhelming odds (no one can achieve such dizzying heights while facing near-death crises many a time in one's journey without grit, iron will and raw courage) take that fateful call to end his life? Was it the short-sighted institutions who turned money lenders and breathed down his neck? He says in his note left behind that one private equity investor, a friend, pushed him to the point of no return and he couldn't take it any longer. Was that, combined by 'tremendous pressure from other lenders', to use his words, that pushed him over the brink? Was the tipping point the tax authorities that he has named? His parting words are so honourable, touching and poignant: 'My intention was never to cheat or mislead anybody…' He ends the letter by saying that his assets (exceeding liabilities) can be used to repay everybody. Such uprightness even while embracing death.

We all wear a mask, maybe even different masks on varying occasions. One we wear for the public. We wear another even when we are with close friends and kith and kin. 'Every man has three personalities, which he exhibits, which he has and that which he thinks he has,' said Alphonse Karr.

If we can sometimes be without the facade? If only Siddhartha had realized he didn't need a mask. If he had sought refuge in someone, a kindred soul, and poured his heart out when the world was unfair to him and he felt let down? If he had only realized that he had already won by innovating a new market in the beverage consumer space where none existed before? If it had just dawned on him that he had hugely succeeded in creating a new cultural space for the young of today to meet and exchange their ideas through his coffee outlets, that he didn't have to prove anything to anybody, he would be with us today.

Before Coffee Day, even in the south, the middle class went to Udupi hotels to read papers over coffee and chat and sip coffee with friends. The Udupi hotels were the favourite hangout places for

Kannada writers. The journalists and writers of the English press went to a few select coffee houses in the cantonment area. The modern youth never visited them.

Siddhartha changed all that – the entire cultural landscape – through his ubiquitous coffee shops, both in the south and the rest of India, where very few drank coffee and spent hours over books or laptops or in simply unwinding with friends.

There is no bigger peak to conquer and no bigger or better glory than what Siddhartha had already achieved, even if he had walked away from his empire to square off his debts. His legacy would have lived on.

CNBC TV18, August 2019

# Retro Tax Was the Art of Luring, Laying a Booby Trap on Investors

The retrospective tax law, a draconian government overreach, enacted by the Congress-led UPA II in 2012, born out of hubris and a twisted sense of sovereignty, was given a formal burial by the BJP-led NDA government through the introduction of a new bill in the Lok Sabha on 5 August 2021.

It may have brought some sense of relief to weary investors who can never predict the wayward ways of our bureaucracy that has perfected the art of laying booby traps to snare unsuspecting investors after luring them into India. Prime Minister Narendra Modi, in his inimitable penchant for pithy slogans, had accused the Congress of 'tax terrorism' during the run up to the 2014 elections that catapulted him to power. The BJP vowed then to scrap the tax if it came to power, but developed selective amnesia soon after winning the elections.

## The background

The venerable late Pranab Mukherjee, former president of India and then finance minister under UPA II, must squarely take the rap for enacting what came to be known as the retrospective taxes in 2012, which sought to tax transactions on transfer of shares of companies outside the country whose assets are in India, going back fifty years till 1962. He could have as well gone back to the time of the East India Company in 1776.

Laurence J. Peter, in his eponymous book *The Peter Principle*, espoused a curious theory that became famous. He states, 'Every employee eventually rises to his level of incompetence.'

Some organizations recognize incompetence and take appropriate action: they simply fire the person from the post. Many do not or cannot due to the person's loyalty to the organization or perceived indispensability and, in some cases, emotional attachment. Laurence says that in such instances they are simply kicked upstairs to posts like vice presidents, where they are imprisoned in ceremonial trappings so that they are out of the way.

There was general consensus that Mukherjee wrecked the economy and undid all that the UPA had accomplished under Prime Minister Manmohan Singh and former Finance Minister P. Chidambaram. Despite the scandals and coalition-induced paralysis, the economy had raced ahead, riding on India's entrepreneurial energy.

Many alleged that Mukherjee as the finance minister was unable to grasp the ramifications of his acts on investor sentiments and their impact on the economy, and was unable to rein in his bunch of well-meaning but misguided bureaucrats who committed hara-kiri.

The Congress, at the Congress Working Committee meeting, alarmed at the negative publicity and flak it drew from the international community and the tailspin of the economy because of retrograde policies, openly castigated the policies of the finance ministry – and by implication, the minister in charge. Even then many feared the worst, which eventually came to pass: the Congress may be routed in the 2014 general elections.

The irony was not lost on anyone: the erstwhile architect of India's reforms, Manmohan Singh, as the head of government, watched mutely.

It is not easy to fix the economy of a country. 'If all the economists were laid end to end, they would never reach a conclusion,' said George Bernard Shaw. In this case, it looked as though the finance ministry was being blamed not so much for its lacklustre performance but for being hell-bent on derailing the economy, which was robust and growing at a fast clip.

Mukherjee was widely respected, without any taint and suave. He had an endearing personality and a Machiavellian mind and was adept at deftly navigating the minefields of politics. He was cultured and statesmanlike and had always delivered on his mission as a troubleshooter.

Elevating Mukherjee was a masterstroke. The Congress had discovered the Peter Principle long before Laurence J. Peter. Was it not the Congress that invented the easy way of getting rid of ministers by rewarding them with governorships? But Mukherjee's stature was so towering that there was only one post for him: The President of India. He was put out of harm's way in pomp and splendour at the Rashtrapati Bhavan.

## The present

It still beats one why the Modi government, which after rightly attacking the Congress on its regressive and bizarre retrospective tax policy, was as bull-headed as the Congress in continuing with the policy and hounding Vodafone and Cairn Energy UK (now Capricorn Energy)? Why did it take seven years to dawn on the current government that it was axing the trunk of its economy by going back on its election promises – and that too after Modi aggressively wooed investors during his foreign visits to invest in India.

With international tribunals awarding judgments in favour of Vodafone, Cairn and also Devas Antrix in an unrelated case, India increasingly came across in poor light as an unreliable partner, disrespecting and violating not only its Supreme Court judgments but also disregarding international bilateral treaties, which are the bedrock of trade and commerce.

The ‘retro tax’ was ill-starred from the time it was hatched in the UPA finance ministry and enacted. It is never late to allow prudence to triumph over obduracy and skewed sense of sovereignty. The current government’s action to scrap it has to be welcomed. Let this commendable gesture open the floodgates of more sensible reforms in the near future.

However, one still wonders why the government did not show grace and accept the international tribunal awards in *toto*, which was in consonance with the Supreme Court verdict. The government could have put a lid on it once and for all, instead of allowing loose ends still open for possible litigation, by accepting the award without reservations and qualifications that the tax demand will be waived and refunds would be made where applicable only if the petitioners withdraw claims on interest, penalties, litigation costs and damage, retaining only the caveat that they must withdraw all cases against the government to benefit from the amendment. Magnanimity to those who have been ill-treated and suffered huge losses and had to fight for justice in international forums, will far outweigh any penny-pinching and arm-twisting to withhold the tribunal awards.

Let me narrate an apocryphal story that may hold a moral. The late Ramakrishna Hegde, commerce minister during A.B. Vajpayee’s NDA government, had come as chief guest to launch my helicopter base in New Delhi. When I bemoaned the bureaucratic red tape and harassment faced by entrepreneurs, he regaled the audience with this story: A few tourists from the West were visiting some famous Hindu temples. As they entered a temple, the guard stopped them and asked them to leave their shoes there. They were surprised. They were barefoot. They said they had already left their shoes in the car. The guard pointed to a board next to him, which said, ‘Leave your shoes here’, and claimed that they could not be left in the car!

The long arm of the law and the mind of the bureaucrat can, at will, make a heaven of hell and a hell of heaven.

Can we expect a change in mindset in the coming years?

*Moneycontrol*, August 2021

# Why Are the Tatas So Crazy About Air India?

Air India! The name, in the 1950s, 1960s and 1970s, during the days of the Licence Raj, conjured images of exotic destinations, distant glitzy cities and mystic lands. It had romance. If you frequently travelled by Air India for work or vacations, it conveyed that you had arrived in society. You belonged to a swish set of people.

It was an exclusive world that exuded discreet power and spelt high society, glamour and wealth. If you had a job in Air India as a pilot, you were the most eligible and sought-after bachelor. If you were an air hostess, you were a young goddess in the skies as unattainable as an Urvashi. That was then, when J.R.D. Tata ran the airline.

Today it's a doddering, decrepit, down-and-out airline with an overstaffed, disgruntled and dowdy crew. Few opt to fly the airline either on domestic or international routes. It is perceived as an unreliable and shabbily managed airline. It is another government department that has piled astronomical debt and continues to bleed cash every day; those who run it are unable to stop the losses. If you have a job there, you may be embarrassed to share your business card.

The Tatas won the Air India bid for ₹18,000 crore. That is not all. The Tatas have to retain all the 13,500 employees for one year and take on the load of retrenching the redundant staff with an attractive VRS scheme that will add additional burden to the sky-high debt.

Then there's the Herculean task of re-engineering and re-equipping many of the grounded aircraft, which have been robbed of parts. They have to be liveried, refurbished and spruced up. That will take up a lot of cash and time and haemorrhage more cash as they sit on the ground.

One wonders why any sane person would wish to sink tens of thousands of crores of rupees to acquire a broken airline when it would take an average of ₹350–400 crore (the amount invested to start IndiGo) to launch a new airline and less than what Rakesh Jhunjhunwala has invested for Akasa. Why are the Tatas so crazy about Air India when they already have a controlling stake in two other carriers – AirAsia and Vistara – which are also bleeding heavily since they were launched five years ago. The Tatas may have once owned Air India that shone like a jewel in their firmament, but does it matter when most of the current generation of Indians are unaware that the Tatas ever owned it?

The Tatas are at heart entrepreneurs and great empire builders. The first seed of that empire was sown by Jamsetji Tata more than 150 years ago. A great visionary, India's first Prime Minister Jawaharlal Nehru likened him to a 'one man planning commission'. Like many empires, they have risen and fallen, and risen again. When steel prices stumbled after World War I and Tata Steel was under severe financial crisis facing closure, Sir Dorabji Tata pledged his wife's jewellery and personal assets to raise loans from banks to pay salaries of employees. When kings at times lose one of their precious principalities or possessions, no price is too high to repossess it. Such entrepreneurs are rare now.

J.R.D. Tata was respected as a visionary business leader and was revered for his humanitarian and charitable work through the Tata Trusts, a legacy he inherited from Jamsetji Tata and his son Dorabji Tata. He was also looked up to as an intrepid aviator and as the man who built a great and popular airline with an impressive national and international network.

J.R.D. was India's first licensed pilot in 1929. He also flew the first commercial flight in 1932 that was carrying airmail from Karachi to Madras via Ahmedabad, Bombay, Poona, Kolhapur, Bellary and Bangalore, in a single-engine tiny three-seater unpressurized de Havilland Puss Moth. This was the beginning of Tata Airlines, which was eventually renamed Air India in 1946 when it became a limited company.

J.R.D. was an extraordinary and daring entrepreneur. Though he founded TCS, Tata Motors, Titan, Tata Salt, Voltas and Air India, the airline was the closest to his heart, and he nourished and cherished it. He was twenty-eight when he flew that flight carrying mail in 1932 and gave wings to Air India. He was forty-nine when it was 'stolen' from him by Nehru (then Prime Minister), who was also his friend. It was not only the crown jewel of the Tatas; it was India's pride.

Still hurting from that loss, the Tatas, under the stewardship of Ratan Tata, attempted to re-enter the aviation space when successive governments opened up the sector to private players along with dismantling the Licence Raj. The Tatas' attempts were thwarted earlier not only by entrenched players such as Jet Airways but also by Air India. A mocking irony.

Now, not long after the Tatas launched two airlines (AirAsia and Vistara), the Narendra Modi government put up for auction a debt-ridden Air India. Ratan Tata, a passionate aviator and entrepreneur extraordinaire cast in the mould of J.R.D., now at the helm of affairs but still hurting and humiliated by what the Government of India had done to the Tatas, is resolved to bring back Air India.

Only cold analysts can fault such an insane decision. Who can put a value to that emotion, that haunting nostalgia and mystique of that lost diamond that is still alluring to the Tata scion? Air India is still a much-loved brand with immense value of bilateral rights and network and infrastructure. The Tatas' war chest is loaded. For example, a sale of one per cent of the shares of TCS (a company built under Ratan Tata's reign) will fetch around ₹14,500 crore.

However, things can nosedive at a rapid pace. When Air Deccan was losing money, I once remarked that my cheques flew faster than my planes. That said, this may seem an impossible dream, but it's doable and a worthy challenge.

The pitfalls are many and real. There are now three airlines in the Tata kitty. Merging the three entities will result in huge cost savings of reduced employees and infrastructure by eliminating three separate CEOs with three boards of directors and similarly three departments each of finance, engineering, operations, IT, revenue management, etc. It will prevent the three airlines competing with each other and cannibalizing each other's passengers instead of competing as one major carrier against IndiGo, Spice and GoAir. If the airlines can put aside their ego and convert all domestic routes to single-class all-economy on the lines of Air France and other major European carriers and keep business class and economy only on international flights, the Tatas might just be able to pull it off and compete against the giants such as SIA, Emirates, British Airways and Lufthansa.

They must bear in mind that no full-service carrier has succeeded against low-cost carriers in the domestic market anywhere in the world. The full service is an inherently flawed model.

The three Tata airlines do not have a cultural fit. There are partnership dissonances between the Tatas and Tony Fernandes of AirAsia, who still holds shares, and between Singapore Airlines and Vistara. All this needs lightning speed and the ability to fuse the three entities into a single homogenous, tight-knit, vibrant company with a common heartbeat and vision.

Ratan Tata is in his eighties, and N. Chandrasekaran, the chairman of Tata Sons who wants to rebuild Air India to its glory days, has no time to lose. He must find the right man to lead Air India – someone who has the heart and brains of J.R.D. – if he has to deliver on his promise to make it a jewel of the Tata Group and a pride of India again.

No one seems on the horizon.

*Moneycontrol*, January 2022

# Where Is the Tata Who Can Restore It to Glory?

Paris, prince of Troy, stole Helen, the wife of King Menelaus of Sparta. Menelaus led a war against Troy, killing Paris. Helen's beauty inspired Christopher Marlowe to gush, 'Was this the face that launched a thousand ships … Sweet Helen, make me immortal with a kiss.' Whether Helen wished to return to her husband is a matter of conjecture, but the romance of waging a war to repossess a stolen bride continues. On a less heroic scale, Air India, an enchanting bride, was snatched from the Tata empire through nationalization in 1953. While one can imagine what passions drive men to wage war to repossess the women they loved, one wonders what possessed Ratan Tata to retrieve Air India, now an impoverished relict.

J.R.D. Tata, the passionate founder of Air India and its chairman until 1977, competed against legendary international airlines – Pan Am, American, United from the US; British Airways, Air France, Lufthansa from Europe; and Japan Airlines, Cathay and Qantas from the East – and earned fulsome praise for operational efficiency and reliability, winning customers. It was no mean achievement. But J.R.D. overtook them in service excellence. He created a distinctive identity and an aura that surrounded the airline. Long before

Singapore Airlines created the iconic Singapore Girl, Air India's air hostesses in their fine silk sarees embodied India's unique, vibrant and diverse culture – sophisticated yet traditional, with understated elegance and grace.

J.R.D. was a towering figure. It is well known that he was India's first licensed pilot in 1929. In 1932, he flew India's first commercial flight, carrying mail and two passengers from Karachi to Chennai via Mumbai on a single-engine hopping flight. That saw the birth of Tata Airlines, which became Air India in 1946. It was a pioneering feat.

But what is less known is that he was a daredevil. In 1930, Prince Aga Khan announced an air race for Indian nationals. The winner of the first solo flight from England to India, or vice versa, to be completed within six weeks from the start, would receive a prize. J.R.D. took the challenge, and so did two other intrepid pilots – Manmohan Singh from Rawalpindi and Aspy Engineer, who had just turned eighteen. The latter two took off separately from Croydon, England. J.R.D. embarked on his flight from Karachi in the opposite direction. Manmohan damaged his aircraft en route but managed to reach Karachi after six weeks.

Feisty Aspy Engineer, who later became the second chief of the Indian Air Force, had a snag while flying across Europe and landed at the remote Aboukir airstrip in the desert near Alexandria in Egypt, needing spark plugs. J.R.D. lost his way due to a faulty compass, zigzagged via Haifa and Cairo and also landed at Aboukir and ran into his competitor Aspy. The inherent magnanimity of J.R.D. came to the fore. Both were flying Gipsy Moths. Without a thought, J.R.D. gifted Aspy four of his spare spark plugs, which he had kept for himself as reserve for any eventuality. And soon, both took off in opposite directions and reached their destinations. Aspy won the Aga Khan Prize, beating J.R.D. by two-and-a-half hours. Imagine their grit, flying through thunderstorms, high turbulence and fog, over mountains and deserts, with just a map and compass. GPS did not exist then.

J.R.D. combined in himself the magical qualities that make a great leader. Vision, magnanimity, charity, insight, decisiveness in complex situations, courage, talent for grooming younger people and immense charisma.

While J.R.D. also showed remarkable entrepreneurial foresight and set up Tata Motors, Titan, TCS, Voltas and Air India, he founded institutions like the Tata Memorial Centre for Cancer Research and Treatment, Tata Institute of Social Sciences and Tata Institute of Fundamental Research – which together enhanced the fortunes and the image of the Tatas, and of India.

But what were the unique traits that distinguished him to build a great airline that was both successful and popular?

J.R.D. could see the big picture and yet never lost sight of the finer details. He would walk the aisles, converse with passengers, make meticulous notes and follow up with letters to departmental heads. On flights, he would wipe any stains on the coffee cups and jugs. He once went into the lavatory, rolled up his sleeves and scrubbed the toilet. The airline staff got the message. With his intuitive Parisian taste for elegance (his mother was French, and he grew up in France as a child), he took great interest in the design of cabin ambience and in the attire and coiffure of the air hostesses (which never appeared like uniforms); he paid attention to the cuisine and the music that wafted through the cabin, which enchanted passengers as they came on board. With flights on time and flawless operations, Air India became the true pride and brand ambassador for the new nation that had just emerged from its dark past.

Ratan Tata's achievements are considerable. He transformed the Tatas into a global behemoth after taking over from J.R.D., acquiring companies like Tetley, Jaguar, Land Rover and Corus Steel. But when you look at the recent acquisition of Air India, which is drowning in debt while two of his other airlines are also haemorrhaging cash, you begin to wonder if he is chasing a mirage, carried away by sentiment and ego in repossessing an ideal that no longer exists. It's a starkly different world today from the J.R.D. era.

The present generation of leaders at the helm of affairs at the Tata companies were all born after the 1950s and were in their late twenties when J.R.D. was 'sacked' as chairman of Air India by the Janata Party (although he returned to it briefly after Indira Gandhi returned to power). None of them have first-hand experience of the great leadership and managerial qualities of J.R.D., save for Ratan Tata, who was groomed under him, but who is now eighty-four. We all romanticize the past, but who among the phalanx of leaders in the Tata Group can fill the shoes of J.R.D. to overcome what seems like an insurmountable challenge from the likes of IndiGo, SIA and Emirates? Can an external professional CEO pull it off?

Air India is now in the kitty. The Tatas must move with lightning speed. The challenges seem daunting. But everything is possible. As Walt Disney said, 'If you can dream it, you can do it.'

*Deccan Herald*, October 2021

# Basking in Reflected Glory

'Wow!' I said when news flashed that one more Indian, Parag Agrawal, from one of the Indian Institutes of Technology (IITs), had been appointed the CEO of Twitter, a global technology behemoth that is shaping opinions, politics and the lives of people around the world. Is this a cause for joy? Did the hearts of Indians swell with pride? Indeed. Which parent won't rejoice at such an achievement? Is there any alma mater that will not be proud of students like Mr Agrawal?

## A mass exodus

Yet, there was something troubling, a vague disquiet about this achievement. Can India rightfully bask in the reflected glory of those who left its shores and rose to the very pinnacle of their profession in a foreign land? Is this not the United States' achievement? Is it not the fertile ecosystem of the United States that helps spot talent and allows people to rise to the top? The United States has its dark spots, but it holds a promise to millions, even penniless immigrants, that they can achieve their wildest dreams if they reach there. It is this America of opportunities that has beckoned millions of migrants over two centuries – not just Indians, but people from every nook and corner of the world.

Mr Agrawal's journey has been similar to that of many Indians before him who we have admired over the years. Many CEOs are from the IITs and other well-known engineering colleges of India. After graduation, they headed to the United States and graduated from prestigious universities like Harvard, MIT, Stanford, and Cornell. Indra Nooyi (PepsiCo), Sundar Pichai (Alphabet and Google), Satya Nadella (Microsoft), Arvind Krishna (IBM), Ivan Menezes (Diageo), Vasant Narasimhan (Novartis), Punit Renjen (Deloitte) and Ajay Banga (Mastercard) are some of those who rose to the pinnacle of their companies. There are thousands of successful techies in smaller companies who also migrated to lead a gilded life.

Technology dominates our business and life. Those who lead tech companies are the new rock stars and demigods of the modern world. They have eclipsed the old-world magnates of steel, oil and automobiles – men like Paul Getty, Andrew Carnegie and Henry Ford. But there are also other Indian migrants who have distinguished themselves in the United States in the fields of management education, science, medicine and economics, among others. The number of leading physicians in medical schools and hospitals, investment bankers and professors in academia boggles the mind. But the loftiest stars among them are the Indian-origin Nobel laureates in physics, chemistry, medicine and economics who pursued their higher education in the United States and settled there.

The troubling question is, why do our brightest minds fly to the West soon after graduation, especially to the United States? The exodus from our premier institutions started in the late 1960s when private sector companies were few, and there were few good jobs available in staid public sector undertakings. The government provided only a few hundred coveted positions each year in the Indian Foreign Service, Indian Administrative Service and Indian Police Service. The rest joined revenue and allied services and lower-level grades which offered security and sinecure.

The exodus continues. Even as we fellow Indians feel a sense of pride at the prosperity of the Indian community in the States, we cannot but help feel a tinge of sadness too. India, even after over seven decades of independence, is mired in poverty and inequality, while our most gifted head for the West.

When non-resident Indians – accomplished economists, scientists or CEOs – lecture India on what it should do to become a developed economy or how it should achieve equitable growth to alleviate poverty, there is a widespread feeling that they have lost their rights to give us such advice, even if it is sincere and well-intended, as they don't live here. We who live here have to fight our battles and our injustice and make India a better place.

## An insecure diaspora

But there is another lot of Indians too, millions of ordinary ones, largely in the United States, who, cut off from their moorings and culture, turn inwards by building temples and forming regional as well as religious associations. This is an insecure diaspora that is not fully assimilated into the adopted westernized society and also alienated from its Indian roots. These non-resident Indians (NRIs) have become more and more jingoistic and find false pride in spreading fake messages about ancient Hindu mythology – messages that Indians invented plastic surgery or rocketry or aeroplanes much before the West – and exhorting Hindus in India to be proud of their heritage and religion and guard against becoming a minority in their own nation. In doing so, they forget that they themselves are a minority in an alien land. At times like this, we feel a tinge of shame.

Seshadri Kumar, an IIT graduate from Bombay, with an MTech and PhD from the States, who returned to India, wrote recently in *The Wire* that it is not surprising that a 'dozen of the top CEOs in the world come from a country with 18% of the world's population'. He wrote, 'So forgive me if I don't join the celebrations. But you know who should really be proud. The Chinese. Because Chinese people did not need to go to the U.S. to rise to the top. They were able to create success stories for themselves sitting in China. And unlike Indians, who are merely CEOs of companies founded by Americans, like Google, Microsoft and Twitter, the Chinese entrepreneurs founded world beating companies in China – Alibaba, Tencent, Didi, Xiaomi, Great Wall Motors, Huawei, ZTE, Foxconn and many others. When Indians do that, I'll join the party.'

That should wake up policymakers. What is India doing wrong? The greater glory is not in training engineers to become CEOs in the United States but in enabling a conducive ecosystem in India that creates world-beating companies and in building institutions that can produce Nobel laureates. How can India create a climate that will prevent its best minds from going to foreign lands? The United States, a nation of immigrants, is a capitalist, market-driven democracy. China is a communist country that has embraced capitalism along with authoritarianism and snuffed out freedom. Both have built a great economy and eliminated poverty. Which of these should India emulate? How can it progress while preserving its diversity and vibrant democracy? Should we not feel remorse that we have failed our youth who do not see a future here and fly to the States after graduation? Shouldn't we reflect on our own migrants and minorities and on their status in our society? Perhaps India is poor not because of a lack of resources or for want of talent but because of its policies, polity and politics.

*The Hindu*, December 2021

# How to Bring Back Hope: Fair, Stable and Socially Moderate Policies are a Prerequisite for Economic Revival

Strong leaders bristle at criticism. Therefore it was a nice surprise when Prime Minister Narendra Modi, at an inaugural public function of Rajasthan Patrika Gate recently, observed that criticism in the era of social media is natural and can strengthen democracy. I'm taking him at his word and sharing some thoughts on the ailing economy and what steps he may need to take to create an ecosystem for reviving it.

Earlier in January this year, Modi met some business leaders in New Delhi – the usual lot who also used to meet the UPA leaders. The exercise was intended to get feedback from the tycoons on the state of the economy, already in the doldrums then, before Covid plunged it to abysmal depths. Our business leaders – who sing paeans even when a lacklustre Budget is presented – spoke of the usual things: credit squeeze, stimulating demand, tax terrorism, simplifying GST, monetary policies, fiscal deficits and so forth.

What wasn't said in the various PM's meetings was more important than what was conveyed – the need for Modi to focus on fixing the trust deficit between government and sections of India's civil society. He should have been told that the present rightwing politics which is continually stirring the communal pot, isn't enabling the ecosystem of social harmony to prevail.

This isn't to give a clean chit to rabid groups on the left, but to point out that the Union government must act firmly, swiftly and justly against zealots and fanatics acting illegally on both sides of the social and political divide, and to bridge the chasm between pro-government cheerleaders and anti-government protesters, where current politics invariably overrides rule of law.

India Inc, in its frequent interactions with the PM, should drive home the simple fact that peace and stability are a prerequisite to getting the economy back on track, and that needs to be in place before administering any medicines for the country's economic ills.

The economy can't be fixed by enabling the rise of stocks of a few companies that take average indices to a high. We can't achieve meaningful development worth its name if there's perennial social strife. India Inc must stop behaving like ostriches, restricting itself to seek policy benefits. During the years of racist conflict in America, Emerson said, 'trade is a plant which always grows wherever there's peace, as soon as there's peace, and as long as there's peace.'

Businesses in general (and even businesses of crony capitalists) can't prosper in isolation over the long term if there's widespread and prolonged inequity and constant friction and conflict in society – conflicts of class, caste and religion, resulting in the collapse of the rest of the economy. When a ship sinks, all aboard perish.

Now for some candid admissions and stark truths. Our big business tycoons are a bigger threat to the growth of a liberal economy than politicians, because they want to do away with competition, harking back to our 'licence raj' days of Ambassador cars. Once they reach the top they forget it was reforms that catapulted them to those dizzy heights.

Individual business houses lobbying in the shadows to secure special dispensations and garner unfair competitive advantage over others, including multinationals, are at cross purposes with Modi's grand vision of 'Make In India' and in conflict with his ambitious plans of attracting FDI and moving up the ladder of ease of doing business.

Investors come to India captivated by the India growth story, and after being wooed by the PM and state leaders when they meet them during their overseas trips. After they invest, if they discover that policies are changed at will to suit local business tycoons and rules are interpreted by clever bureaucrats who lay booby traps and make it difficult for them to grow, then future foreign investments will dry up. It will also shake the confidence of local industry.

Amazon and Walmart are already crying foul. In effect, foreign companies feel that doing business in India depends on who you know. It's a snakes and ladders game. When governments renege on their promises and promote some business houses over others, the economy will be adversely affected, and entrepreneurial spirit will evaporate. There will also be retaliation on our exports and on businessmen who invest abroad.

It's not easy to steer the economy of a large complex country where multiple contrasting Indias – islands of prosperity in a vast sea of poverty and ignorance – coexist. When the country is faced with threats on three fronts – a plummeting economy, the Covid virus, and a belligerent China on our borders – the PM must surround himself with the best minds from around the world. And there's no dearth of them. Hence his eagerness to engage with critics has to be lauded.

By virtue of the mandate he commands, both in the country and within his party, it behoves Modi – as the leader of the largest democracy that aspires to be among the prosperous nations of the world – to reach out and unite a currently polarised nation. He must bring back hope. Hope that things will mend no matter how tough the times are now, hope that the future holds promise. Hope, the invisible fuel of an economy, seems absent now.

Because, no matter how noble or correct the intentions, no shop can do good business in a bad neighbourhood.

*The Times of India*, September 2020

# Axing the Economy's Trunk

It is hard to come to grips with the calamity that unfolded before our eyes on our television screens over the past few weeks, of hundreds of thousands of migrants pouring out of arterial roads of our metros across the country, walking for days with tired limbs and calloused feet, with just one desperate cry: 'Take us home.' How could we reconcile ourselves to this cruel and conspicuous irony – a strong and muscular nation aiming to be a $5-trillion economy mutely watching a refugee crisis of monumental proportions?

We have our blemishes and our injustices, but we have always taken pride in being a great vibrant democracy because we are constantly striving to redeem ourselves, 'to wipe every tear from every eye'. Yet, we seem inept and appear to be bumbling as we watch from the cosy confines of our homes the never-ending, long, arduous march of hungry millions. So, what went wrong? Did our government fail our poor ? Tagore's lines of penetrating insight come to mind: 'The world suffers most from the disinterested tyranny of the well wisher … the clumsiness of power spoils the key, and uses the pickaxe.' Did our politicians and bureaucrats use a pickaxe when they could have used a key? Is it possible that unwittingly, our policies and decisions to impose the lockdown were seen only through the eyes of the middle class?

## A 140 million–strong workforce

The migrants are ubiquitous. Their numbers are staggering – 100 million migrant labourers spread across our large metros and another forty million resident daily wage earners engaged in various vocations. They are the construction workers, courier boys, taxi drivers, painters, carpenters, security guards, cooks, maids, vegetable vendors and service providers of every kind imaginable, who keep us well-provided, happy and warm. Our agriculture today, in the peak seasons of harvest and sowing, depends largely on migrants. They put food on our table. They are the warp and woof of our society. This free flow and migration in such large numbers from one state to another is the true validation of our vibrant economy and affirmation of our multi-ethnic and diverse society. They are the very spirit and heartbeat of India. The medium- and small-scale industries and the self-employed proprietary businesses at the bottom of the period, as also the construction industry in our metros, would collapse without this voiceless, nameless army of migrants. The micro, small and medium enterprises and migrant workers contribute 40 per cent to our GDP. So why are we axing the trunk of our economy?

Governments at the state and the Centre are guilty, but we the people, who have partaken of every benefit from the sweat and labour of these millions of migrants, cannot exculpate ourselves either. The altruism of many of us to feed the hungry, while laudable, will not give them back their dignity. They have lost their dwellings and livelihoods and, along with it, their dignity.

## A functioning anarchy

Further, our problems are different, unique and complex, with our teeming migrant populations living cheek by jowl in their tenements and overcrowded alleys, needing work every day to feed themselves. We are not Europe or the United States or even China, where the back-end ecosystem is robust, well-structured and organized. We are in the main a largely chaotic people, undisciplined and disorganized. But we are very enterprising and innovative. Beneath all this chaos and confusion and mad disorder, there is a vibrant shadow economy that miraculously keeps buzzing and ticking. Economist and former US Ambassador to India, John Kenneth Galbraith, said sixty years ago that 'India is a functioning anarchy.' We still are. So, let's remember what works for poor people in the West will not work for us here. We must find our own solutions that address both lives and livelihoods.

The government must find every which way to send all the migrants home swiftly, free of cost. And it should plan well and find ways to open the economy and regain the trust of the migrant workforce, without whose participation the economy is unlikely to bounce back.

*The Hindu*, June 2020

# Seal GST with a KISS: 'Keep It Simple, Stupid' Should Be the Watchword for GST Reform

The late Finance Minister Arun Jaitley had announced in December 2018 that the sun would soon set on the 28 per cent GST slab, except for luxury items. The country could look forward eventually to only two slabs – 5 per cent and a standard rate between 12 per cent and 18 per cent (apart from exempt items). But he did not make haste and, tragically, death overtook him prematurely in less than a year. He could not fulfil his assurances.

GST is still a complicated tax regime with varying slabs, not easy to comprehend or comply with, and open to interpretation, harassment and avoidable litigation. Finance ministry officials can be reminded of the KISS principle again.

KISS – Keep It Simple, Stupid – is a well-known acronym and an accepted credo in business. It is attributed to Lockheed aircraft engineer Kelly Johnson, who used it to urge his engineers to keep the aircraft design so simple that even a stupid person should be able to repair the aircraft with ordinary tools on the combat field.

Bureaucracy, the world over, is usually oblivious to the KISS principle. An Amazon advertisement boasts that it sells more than a crore different products, besides myriad services, with more categories added every day. In this context, asking bureaucrats to identify and categorize all products and services for differential tax slabs in the GST regime is the surest way to get into a muddle.

Empirical data from across the world on the benefits of a unified single tax is incontrovertible. So, an unambiguous directive to the bureaucracy is necessary to come up with just two categories: Goods eligible for zero tax, and all the rest to come under a single rate, say 10 per cent or 12 per cent or even lower. That means everything, except specifically exempt goods, is taxed.

This needs bold and clear reformist thinking at the political level. Take the so-called 'sin' taxes. They make no sense and are at cross purposes with government's overarching policies of generating growth and creating jobs under the much-touted 'Make In India'.

A typical 300-room five-star hotel generates direct employment for around 500 people, 90 per cent of whom are waiters, housekeeping staff, front desk and concierge staff, cooks, chefs, managers and financial and clerical staff. There are a host of others employed in associated services such as the spa, gift shops and swimming pool. The hotel also generates indirect employment in ancillary areas: It buys bed linen, furnishings, rugs and carpets (that are periodically replaced, generating employment in textiles), air conditioners, cutlery, electrical fittings, furniture, etc., and consumes enormous quantities of food produce. All these generate jobs and income for farmers, construction contractors, artisans and other manufacturers.

Five-star hotels also generate foreign exchange by attracting rich tourists and visitors and have a direct bearing on foreign direct investment (FDI). So, it is unwise to tax these hotels to death. It is the same warped view that has high taxes on air conditioners, air-conditioned restaurants, chocolates or luxury cars. They create an economic ripple effect downstream, in a complex web of businesses that have symbiotic relationships reaching down to the bottom of the employment pyramid.

One must figure out how to rev up the economy by making the rich and upper middle class spend and moving more people up the value chain to buy more chocolates, air conditioners and automobiles, instead of designing a tax system that keeps these products out of the new consumer class's reach.

Similarly, in a roadside bakery, for example, officials have excelled in the art of creating confusion – bread has zero tax, but a vegetable sandwich is in the 5 per cent tax slab, hitting the vegetable grower directly. A bun has zero tax, but a bun with a few raisins is taxed at 5 per cent. And cakes and chocolates are at 18 per cent! It is the same with taxes on wine, rum and beer, which generate large scale employment and are the backbone of grape and sugarcane farming and the cocoa industry.

Take for example the curious case of the GST dispute between the popular start-up iD Fresh Food, which is in the business of ready-to-eat foods like chapatis, rotis and parottas and sells various types of idli and dosa batters. They were selling parottas along with rotis and chapatis and charging 5 per cent GST. A clever tax sleuth came up with a brilliant finding and slapped an 18 per cent GST, arguing that chapati and roti are flatbreads whereas parottas are layered breads and hence do not qualify for the lower tax slab.

Can a country aspire to be a $5 trillion economy if its taxmen turn gourmet chefs and get bogged down into researching types of dough making while start-ups struggle to make dough? The low-cost airline model is successful because of the KISS principle: elimination of all frills – food, water, freebies, assigned seats, etc. They have single-class seating, point-to-point travel with no code sharing, direct internet booking and no middlemen. It's an Udupi self-service hotel in the sky!

The finance minister, instead of moving gingerly as has been the case till now, should take a cue from the Prime Minister, who hinted at major reforms in the aftermath of COVID-19 and do away with all the confusing tax slabs in one fell swoop. She can then usher in a truly single low tax rate along with a list of exempt items. That will ensure compliance, widen the tax net, improve the ease of doing business, boost the economy, create jobs and increase tax collection as witnessed in many countries – a move that will be both populist and well-regarded by economists.

It is well to remember Winston Churchill's famous quip: 'A nation trying to tax itself into prosperity is like a man standing in a bucket and trying to lift himself by the handle.'

*The Times of India*, January 2021

# Unease of Doing Global Business

When the Tatas announced on February 15 that the group had appointed Ilker Ayci as Air India CEO, it took the aviation world by surprise. But not for the reasons for which he declined the job he was to join from April 1 on Tuesday. Ayci was no 'rock star' in aviation circles with a pedigree from iconic airlines from the likes of Delta, American, or legendary low cost South West Airlines from the US or British Airways, Lufthansa or Air France from Europe. In fact, he was largely unknown as CEO of Turkish Airlines, a relatively small airline compared to the biggies but was tasked with the complex merger of the three entities of Air India, Vistara and Airasia – the three airlines in which Tatas now have majority stake, all loss making which he was supposed to lead to profit and eventually bring under one umbrella.

Going by his by no means unimpressive background – which includes turning around Turkish Airlines, quite large compared to Indian carriers, of which he was chairman from 2015 till January 2022 – one wondered if he was the right fit for the daunting task.

That Ilker is a close friend of Recep Erdogan - and was his adviser twice, when the latter was the mayor of Istanbul and again when he became Turkish president – suggested that there could be friction, considering that Erdogan brought up the issue of Kashmir at the UN General Assembly in September 2021, that GoI had termed as 'completely unacceptable'.

The Tatas choosing someone close to politicians was another question. But one thought that the group, with vast experience in dealing with global companies, must have done their homework and were being prudent. On top of that were rumours on social and mainstream media from the likes of the RSS affiliate, Swadeshi Jagran Manch, opposing Ayci's appointment for having 'undesirable links'.

Perhaps realising the atmosphere he was stepping into may not allow him to discharge his role freely, Ayci announced on Tuesday that it was not 'feasible or honourable' for him to accept the position 'in the shadow of such a narrative' in which 'some sections of Indian media' have attempted to 'colour [his] appointment with undesirable colours'.

Social media commentary, flak and even scurrilous rumour-mongering is one thing. Organisations ideologically close to the ruling dispensation of India wishing to subvert the due process of one of India's most trusted industrial houses – and, by extension, the government that made the transition of Air India from PSU to private company possible – is quite another.

The aviation and home ministry rules are crystal clear. All board members and CEOs, COOs and CFOs must have security clearance that are vetted and cleared by all the intelligence agencies before they can be appointed by any airline. The Swadeshi Jagran Manch should have allowed the home ministry to do its job, without fear or favour.

On its part, the Tatas should have stood firm for their right to appoint the best candidates for top jobs in their companies regardless of his or her nationality, ethnicity and religion, subject to laws of the land. They reportedly buckled, for instance, when they pulled out their rather heart-warming advertisement for Tanishq jewellery that showed an interfaith baby shower. Why? Because a section of social media felt it promoted 'love jihad'. Can companies honestly compete globally when they are blackmailed by trolls or agenda-driven NGOs?

Dara Khosrowshahi, an Iranian Muslim immigrant, is the global CEO of Uber in the US, a company that revolutionised the taxi-hailing service. Hamdi Ulukaya is the Greek yogurt king who heads Chobani with a billion-dollar sales in the US. According to the National Foundation for American Policy, 51% US tech unicorns have at least one immigrant at the leadership level. Two of the three most valuable companies in the world are led by US immigrants from India - Microsoft's Satya Nadella, and Google's Sundar Pichai. Parag Agrawàl of Twitter and Shantanu Narayen of Adobe are not seen as 'outsiders' heading these US global giants.

A few years ago, Nadella had said that if India has to compete with US, it must create an ecosystem where a Bangladeshi immigrant one day becomes the CEO of Infosys or any immigrant can set up a unicorn in India. He looked forward to such a day while reminiscing about his own rise to the position of CEO in Microsoft.

We must shed our insecurities, our prejudices and parochialism – and stand up to these in others – if we want India to become a global business and economic powerhouse nation. When India Inc considers hiring talent from overseas, especially from the non Anglo-American sphere - in the case of the Tatas and Air India, from Turkey – we are forgoing best practices and the best talent because of a mix of a colonial hangover and culture of xenophobia.

The Rigveda says, 'Let noble thoughts come to us from all directions.' To that, we can add, 'Let the brightest minds people our land.

*The Economic Times*, March 2022

# SOCIETY AND GOVERNANCE

# An Unequal Battle

The flood of images of devotees – a sea of naked bodies of sadhus and saints at the Kumbh Mela, millions of them, flesh pressing on flesh, masks only on their nether regions, chants issuing out of the gaping cavities in their faces, taking a dip in the Holy Ganga, and then the visuals of hundreds of thousands of people, also crazed devotees, but of their political masters, jostling against each other in election rallies, wide-eyed and open-mouthed with party slogans and war cries of Modi or Didi – made me wonder, can all the reverberating incantations of the sadhus and the rousing exhortations of the politicians save the devotees, their leaders themselves, from the raging virus that is killing indiscriminately?

Putting the noisy television on mute, I watched the images of the silent, jumbled millions and their chanting and haranguing messiahs. It seemed a surreal pantomime, as though a pact had been signed with the devil as they flirted with the virus, a virus that was performing its eerie dance of death. I recalled my first army posting in the jungles and frontier posts of the army in Sikkim and later the Assam-Bengal border.

As a young officer of the regiment, I was made to attend and monitor, by my company commander, the 'machchardani parade' (mosquito net repair parade). Once a month, all jawans were lined up in the courtyard of the barracks, and their mosquito nets were inspected. Those that had holes were repaired by the regimental tailors. I was surprised but also mortified that I was assigned to supervise this pointless parade. 'Did I train at the prestigious National Defence Academy only to do this silly chore?' I thought.

It was also my duty to inspect and ensure that the mosquito nets were drawn down on the beds of jawans at sunset every day. Disregarding this was a punishable offence. My commander, seeing a cynical smirk on my face, did not lecture me but simply gave me a folder on the Burma Campaign and asked me to read it. In the Burma campaign of 1942–43 during World War II, I learnt, the mosquito was more dangerous than the mortar round. Malaria felled and incapacitated more allied soldiers, including thousands of Indian soldiers. This affected more soldiers than even the bullets and artillery shells of the invading Japanese army. I felt deeply embarrassed by my vanity and ignorance.

If such was the rigour with which malaria was fought, why is our response to a virulent virus like the coronavirus, which is decimating people around the world in millions and wreaking havoc on our lives and livelihoods, so cavalier?

Writing in his essay 'Men Versus Insects' nearly ninety years ago, Bertrand Russell presciently wrote, 'Man is safe, except from the little creatures – the insects and the microorganisms. An acre of forest may have more insects and a single animal more microbes than the entire human population. Insects have an advantage over us – they devour our food before it is ripe for us. Microbes are altogether a different mysterious universe. There can be no life or death without microbes.' Even the great scientist Louis Pasteur said, 'Gentlemen, it's the microbes who will have the last word.'

The battle between men and the virus is an unequal battle when people of a country fighting the virus are infected with obscurantism, superstition, jingoism and hubris. We have to cure ourselves of this ailment first. There can be salvation from the virus only through science.

When a society that has a rich civilizational past dives deep into its mythological folklore and finds that the present is in stark contrast to the past, that it has now been scientifically, technologically and developmentally left behind by other advanced economies, it is easy to fall into the trap of worshipping past glories.

It is a convenient way for political and religious leaders, the former promising a utopian future in this world and the latter in the next world, to divert attention away from the present morass the country has sunk into. Such smug wallowing in the past will leave the country deeper in mire and mud. These are not just metaphors. If you were to fall into a bog, no amount of prayers invoking our gods or singing praises to the exploits of our mythic heroes, who had 'mastered plastic surgery', or 'aviation' and 'rocketry', will save us.

The only way to come out of it before being swallowed is to stop being delusional and in denial and recognize the reality and do everything to escape from the bog. Our leaders should face the present honestly, shun all sycophants and courtiers and marshal all data, ensuring that the facts presented to them are not distorted or selectively presented. That is the first step.

And then they must swiftly prepare an action plan to develop capabilities in scaling up vaccination and affordable healthcare infrastructure by consulting the brightest and best minds – doctors, scientists, administrators with integrity; there's no dearth of them – and execute it flawlessly through a task force that continuously monitors the implementation. Dr Prabhat Jha, chair in global health and epidemiology, University of Toronto, said, 'Without data, there is no way for India to walk out of this pandemic. And secrecy in data can only backfire.'

'Man is quite insane. He wouldn't know how to create a maggot, and he creates Gods by the dozen,' said Montaigne, the celebrated French philosopher. We have surpassed all other peoples of the world in creating gods.

*Deccen Herald*, May 2021

# Farm Laws: Reforms by Regressive Ways?

Many of the actions of our governments, both at the Centre and in many states, remind you of an ancient fable about a cock and a cat, attributed to Aesop. The cat is looking for any pretext to make a meal out of the cock. It accuses the cock of disturbing people every morning with its crowing. The cock argues that it is serving the people and its activities benefit society. But the cat ends the dialogue, observing that it is now her breakfast time. 'Cats don't live on dialogue.' Neither do monarchs. But democracies function effectively only through dialogue and discourse.

The three farm laws rammed through Parliament and given presidential assent in a hurry have incurred the wrath of farmers, mainly from Punjab and Haryana, who have been protesting for two weeks and have laid siege to Delhi. Opposition parties across the country and many trade bodies and unions are opportunistically supporting their agitation, reminiscent of when a moribund BJP revived itself by jumping onto the Anna Hazare–led India Against Corruption bandwagon. Now the boot is on the other foot. The ruling party is trying to discredit the farmers, comprising of a large body of sturdy, stout and hearty Sikhs, and attempting to drive a wedge between different farmers' groups.

The farm bills contain far-reaching reforms that could be of benefit to small farmers, who comprise 85 per cent of the farming community. One law unshackles the farmer from the clutches of the APMC mandis and frees him from strangulation by the cartels of brokers and traders in nexus with government inspectors by allowing him to sell where he wants and to whom he chooses anywhere in the country, through physical markets or from his farm gate or via e-markets. The second does away with the Essential Commodities Act and its restrictions on those crops that came under it, allowing greater leeway both in the free movement and storage of produce. The third law is aimed at contract farming directly with farmers and encourages start-ups to innovate and create new markets – domestic and exports – which are presumed to attract massive investments by corporates in procurement, processing and cold storages. These laws together are expected to result in better prices for farmers, by reducing wastage of perishables and increasing competition among buyers, and also to pave way for massive employment in agriculture. The laws do not per se seek to dismantle the APMCs or do away with the Minimum Support Price (MSP). This, in essence, is the premise of the three laws.

Howsoever noble the intentions, though, we know from the past that these issues pertaining to agriculture are so intricate and complex that there is no silver bullet to solve them by just passing ordinances or ramming laws through Parliament. Reforms, to be successful, need continuous tweaking to remove bottlenecks while preventing the formation of cartels.

The three laws are important and are inextricably entwined. They will have far-reaching impacts on farming practices, the livelihood of farmers and farm labourers and supply chain linkages from the farms to retail shelves to your dinner plate. They could turbocharge agriculture start-ups and giant corporates and interconnect the millions of small-time traditional buyers, wholesalers and agents who are all part of the tangled web that will continue to be the backbone of our economy for many years to come.

There are also the ancient weekly village fairs and local markets, as old as our hills, which are probably the best free markets that give access to farmers and artisans to sell their farm produce and vend their pots, baskets and wares, and also help them market their cattle, sheep, poultry and pigs as well as buy their weekly needs. And there are the APMC yards, instituted in the 1960s, which serve a good purpose in a number of states, are absent in a few states and are an anomaly in many other states, having become moribund and cesspools of corruption.

Let us also remember that there are only a limited number of crops that come under the APMC. There are dozens of other crops, fruits and vegetables, flowers and livestock and dairy produce that affect more farmers than those whose crops come under the APMC Act. These crops are not eligible for the government's MSP, and complaints persist that these benefits are not reaching such farmers.

We must recognize that the bills can do enormous good but also have many attendant dangers. Government monopolies like the APMCs are inefficient and indifferent to customers. The private sector, on the other hand, may be efficient, but it is a rapacious, predatory monster. There are legitimate concerns that, let alone multinational corporations (MNCs), Indian corporates and crony capitalists could turn out to be unscrupulous and venal when they become monopolies or form cartels. There is a genuine fear that APMCs may collapse as a result of these laws and farmers will then be at the mercy of large business houses who will eliminate competition and prey on them – a trend that started long ago and has steadily grown, with the increasing influence of a few big business houses on government policy. When procurement through MSP is delayed or denied, farmers under duress will fall into the clutches of corporations run by oligarchs. The unsolved question is, therefore, how to ensure that the reforms do not lead to monopolies or cartelization.

Equally important is the issue of federalism. Agriculture is a state subject under the Constitution, and the states play a critical role in the sector, but they have scarcely been involved in the framing and passing of the laws.

When leaders in the government admit that they may not have all the answers, that no one has a magic formula for societal and economic problems, it will open up avenues for dialogue and debate and lead to faster, amicable and simpler solutions through consensus instead of conflict.

Tagore's lines of penetrating insight may serve us well: 'The clumsiness of power spoils the key and uses the pickaxe.'

*Deccan Herald*, December 2020

# In the Land of Kangaroo Courts, the Law Can Be an Ass

In Charles Dickens's famous novel *Oliver Twist*, Mr Bumble says, 'If the law supposes that, the law is an ass, an idiot.' The law is not only an ass; it is also a bloodhound.

Who among us has not borne the brunt of the idiocy of law? How many may also have been victims of a witch-hunt? The cops who wielded the rifle earlier are now facing the wrath of retaliation by another party.

A home minister hounds another in opposition and sends him to prison. The wheels of fortune turn, and he comes out of jail and takes vengeance when he ascends the throne by imprisoning the former home minister. Justices try themselves in cases of sexual harassment and corruption charges. Lynching in the name of the cow, khap panchayats, Shariat laws, staged police encounters, male chauvinists and priests defying court orders and barring menstruating women from entering temples, judges declaring 'contempt' when someone points out they are violating their own oath of office … the aberrations are not a few in number.

On top of that, the media vultures have taken over an investigation, feasting on a poor dead actor while trying to tear out the flesh of his living, bereaved girlfriend. Are we becoming a country of kangaroo courts with a menagerie of agencies unleashed? Have unbridled bureaucratic power and ridiculous rules and regulations gone berserk?

## A couple of incidents

Let me recall a couple of incidents. When I imported a small nine-seater Swiss Pilatus aircraft from Cape Town in South Africa in 2002, I decided to fly it across Africa and the Middle East to India along with my pilot. The flight over great African forests and mighty deserts promised to be a great adventure. It turned out to be an exhilarating trip but soon ended in a nightmare when we landed at one in the morning at Mumbai airport.

Almost immediately, a customs squad surrounded us and led us to a remote bay. After filling up reams of papers, the customs sleuths suspiciously rummaged the aircraft for any contraband hidden in the plane and finally, at five, the papers were stamped, and we were declared clean. Then we filed a flight plan for Bangalore, and while taxiing to take off around six, a customs jeep along with the airport police rushed to intercept us as we were rolling onto the main runway.

An official came up and said he had forgotten to check the logbook and fuel tank meter to calculate the fuel that was remaining in the tank when we landed from Dubai, our last airport. He said, on that remnant of a few litres of fuel a customs duty had to be paid because it was imported fuel coming into the country. We were led back to the parking bay. We lost a few more hours in this red tape, and by the time we had completed the formalities of paying a couple of hundred rupees in customs duty, the pilot had crossed his flight duty time limitation, and we had to stay put in Bombay for one more day. The official just shrugged his shoulders and said, 'Laws are laws.'

When I narrated this incident during a public launch function of the aircraft in Delhi and bemoaned our asinine laws, the chief guest, Ramakrishna Hegde, the then commerce minister in the A.B.

Vajpayee government and a great raconteur, with a straight face, said, 'Captain, the law is not just an ass, it's a mule at times.'

He then told the story of a group of foreign tourists who were visiting a famous temple in Karnataka. Knowing that visitors could only walk barefoot in the temple, they left their shoes in the car. As they were about to enter, the guard stopped the foreigners, who responded that they had already taken off their shoes. 'The guard said you cannot leave the shoes in your car. And he pointed to a placard which said, "Leave your shoes HERE,"' Hegde ended, amidst laughter. Cleverly and eloquently, Hegde had conveyed the moral of the story to the officials who unfailingly but eagerly applied their rules but rarely applied their minds.

## When law enforcing agencies become handmaidens

Such stories may drive home a point and entertain. But when law enforcing agencies are caught in the vortex of politics and go overboard, either under coercion from political masters or with an eagerness to please them, the story can turn macabre and ruin the lives and wreck the careers of people, as is the case now with the arrest and jailing of Rhea Chakraborty. Allegations ranging from abetment to suicide to murder have now morphed into a narcotics case.

Julio Ribeiro, one of the most venerated former police chiefs, recently said in a television interview, 'The poor girl has sadly become a pawn in the game of rival politicians and overzealous agencies willing to do their masters bidding.' He pointed out that in her impetuosity of youth, she may have erred in procuring drugs for her deceased boyfriend or may have consumed them herself. The narcotic agencies arresting the actress (who is cooperating) in such unseemly haste, instead of focussing on busting the drug cartel and arresting the kingpins of the drug trade who are allegedly supplying Bollywood stars, is a travesty of our justice system.

If the central investigating agencies were seen to be blatantly pandering to the BJP in the Sushant and Rhea case, in the Kangana

Ranaut episode, the Shiv Sena has been brazen, callous and not very intelligent by demolishing her office in swift vigilante retribution for verbally attacking the party and its supremo. True, the actor is known to be provocative and may have been intemperate too. By aligning herself openly with the BJP, she has also exposed herself to charges of nursing political ambitions, making her motives suspect.

But despite that, the Shiv Sena leaders cannot take offence personally and abuse their office, using the state's civic and law enforcement bodies as their private militia to bulldoze Kangana's office. And in one stroke, the Shiv Sena, under the new chief minister, has plundered the goodwill it had earned assiduously over the last year of being a good and impartial administrator overshadowing its former unsavoury reputation of being a fanatical party of hoodlums.

When cases such as the murder of Gauri Lankesh and killings of other rationalists and intellectuals – M.M. Kalburgi, Narendra Dabholkar and Govind Pansare – and the death of Sushant Singh Rajput span two or more states, an overarching oversight by an agency like the CBI and other central agencies may be needed. But can we forget that it is supposed to have a higher fidelity to the oath of office and Constitution, rather than allegiance to a particular ruling party? But how does an accused or victim get justice when the state intelligence and police are seen to be beholden to the ruling party and the central investigating agencies are suspected of being handmaidens of the ruling party at the Centre?

## What the long arm of the law can do

Let me conclude and illustrate what the long arm of the law can do. In the Kannada play of the late and legendary master Hirannaya Lanchavatara – a scathing parody of corruption in our society that ran uninterrupted for six decades – a cop arrests a farmer cycling to a neighbouring village and hauls him to the station. Asked by his inspector what the offence was, the cop replies that the cycle had no lights. The bemused inspector responds, 'But it is broad daylight!' Pat comes the reply, 'True. When I asked the farmer where he was headed, he said he was going to the next hamlet and would be back late at night after his errands. He had no lights mounted, and I imagined he would be riding back when dark without light. So nabbed him to prevent an offence.' The satisfied inspector collects a fine and lets off the farmer.

Even as COVID-19 cases continue to rage and daily deaths mount, the country is facing the worst economic crisis in seventy-five years and the looming threat of war with China, are we so depraved and morbid as to watch unhinged television anchors spewing venom and dishing out Bollywood mush day after day? And are our politicians so callous and irresponsible to neglect matters of state to participate in a witch-hunt against a couple of stars?

*The Wire*, September 2020

# Draconian 'Love Jihad' Laws will Rob Our Young of the Glory of Youth, the Very Essence and Purpose of Life

Love Jihad. What an oxymoron. Even moronically incongruous. As Shakespeare said, 'Doubt truth to be a liar, but never doubt love.'

In my salad days 'when I was young in blood and green in judgment,' and impetuous as a young army officer, myself and two youthful colleagues serving together in a cantonment town were courting three girls who were boarders in a local missionary college. And it so happened one of them, who was seeing me, was a Muslim girl.

Her parents, who were in the Middle East, got wind of it, rushed back to India, grounded her, locked her up in the house and fixed up a boy for marriage post-haste. She called me one day when I was wondering why I had not heard from her for a week and, in desperation, pleaded with me to get her out of her house at night before it was too late, or she would be doomed.

She suggested I arrange to have her secretly lifted out of her room past midnight and send her to her friend, who had a place in Bangalore and agreed to give her board and lodging till she found some job. She was shy of 20 and still an undergraduate. I was in my mid-20s. Marriage was not on our minds.

Young blood danced through our veins, and there was tumult in our hearts. It all did seem 'apparelled in celestial light.' If in youth girls and boys – hearts enflamed and suffused with tender emotions – don't love, what can be more unnatural and unholy?

Coming back to the story, swept away by reckless emotions, imagining myself a white knight to the rescue of a damsel in distress, I went with my buddies at midnight to her house, jumped the high rise compound wall and clambered up to her room on the first floor. We helped her out of the house over the barriers and on to my motorcycle pillion, whisked her away to the railway station and packed her off to Bangalore in the overnight mail train.

When her parents discovered next morning that their daughter had taken flight, all hell broke loose. Police were alerted, and eventually, the girl went back after extracting assurance from her parents that she wouldn't be married off forcibly. I escaped court martial thanks to an army commander who was magnanimous and forgiving.

Luckily the Muslim family never accused me of jihad, or dharmayudh. They were conservative, just as my parents were, and they were not supportive of their children marrying outside their community and their comfort zone.

It's presumptuous and delusional of upper castes to think the families of backward communities and Dalits are happy when a girl or boy marries a Brahmin or a Thakur or a Jat. In the main, they all are as chary of it and don't encourage their children marrying outside their castes and religions. But when the young, on reaching adulthood, fall headlong in love and wish to tie the knot, it's barbaric of elders to come in the way and stop the union of hearts.

Love Jihad is also cruel doublespeak. The campaign by many saffron parties and the UP ordinance is selectively aimed at Muslim boys marrying Hindu girls and not targeted at Hindu boys marrying Muslim girls. It's also perverse logic because Hinduism is resilient and all-embracing and has absorbed influences and enriched itself without losing its core civilisational identity. No other religion has celebrated love in all its many splendoured facets and through its rich mythology, glorified in its temple architecture and other forms of art and literature, Lord Krishna being its pre-eminent deity and beloved symbol of love.

This fear of an imaginary 'love jihad' reflects an insecurity and inferiority complex stemming from a diminutive and dwarfed civilisational outlook that does injustice to a mighty civilisation as imagined by the rest of the world. As the Allahabad High Court commendably said in its November 11 verdict: 'Right to live with a person of his/her choice irrespective of religion professed by them, is intrinsic to right to life and personal liberty. Interference in a personal relationship would constitute a serious encroachment into the right to freedom of choice of the two individuals.'

*The Times of India*, December 2020

# Of Lockdowns and the After-effects

When Emperor Napoleon was once urged by one of his commanders to attack without loss of time, he retorted, 'The Army marches on its stomach.' To fight and win wars, men need timely supplies of food and water as much as the supply backup of ammunition and armament, horses and so forth. In short, good planning and logistics support are vital for victory.

Now, our country is engaged in a different kind of war, one against a raging virus. The overnight lockdown of the whole country on the night of 24 March 2020 was so sudden that people were left shell-shocked. Many daily wage earners who had missed Prime Minister Narendra Modi's television broadcast, or had not grasped the implications of this lockdown, and who ventured out the next morning to work or to buy essentials were mercilessly beaten up by the police.

The decision to impose a total lockdown was a good one and was necessary. The World Health Organization (WHO) recommended it, and the heads of other countries followed suit. That is the only way to stop the spread of the virus. But if the lockdown is to succeed, the supply chain of essential goods and services had to be kept open and running 24x7, and provisions of free cash made to the poor so that people do not defy the orders in search of livelihood.

So, Modi got the first part right – the need for a lightning-fast response and a firm resolve to fight the war. But for the lockdown to be effective, there was a corollary that his team overlooked – a well-planned and efficient supply chain and logistics should have been in place well before the lockdown announcement, one facilitated by authorities at every level and extending to the farthest nook and corner of India, keeping in mind that this is a large, chaotic country. Things work in India haphazardly through local, ad hoc ways, enabled by a complex web of millions of service providers who are on daily wages.

While the middle class can observe social distancing and 'home quarantine', for the millions of daily wage earners who have to buy their provisions or meal daily and can do so only by going to work each day, it is a cruel joke. For such people, it is physically and economically impossible when they are crammed cheek by jowl, seven to eight in a tin shed in densely crowded slums. The total number of resident slum dwellers and economic migrants put together in the large metros and cities is a staggering 110 million. No government can feed them without adequate planning and preparation. It may not even be desirable to lock them down in such extreme conditions.

In the absence of facilities for food and shelter, with the spectre of hunger staring at them, the workers fled from their dwellings, seeking every which way to reach their villages, and spilled out onto highways and bus stands. The heart-rending images of millions of poor, hungry men and women, carrying what they could, with wailing children in tow, are haunting.

While no effort must be spared to stem the spread of the virus, practical solutions that suit India should have been explored and put in place before the imposition of a sudden lockdown. That called for courageous feedback from the advisers to the prime minister, who may have been impatient to enforce the lockdown under counsel from epidemiologists who, in turn, couldn't have foreseen the fall-out of such a sudden lockdown and the collateral damage it would inflict on the poor. The cure suggested is becoming worse than the disease, as we can all see.

Let me recount a story of another war – the Bangladesh War of 1971, images of which are still vivid in my mind as I took part in it. In April 1971, Sam Manekshaw, the then army chief, was summoned to an emergency cabinet meeting by Indira Gandhi and asked if the military was ready to attack East Pakistan as millions of refugees were pouring in through Assam, destabilizing India. Manekshaw resisted. 'I'm not prepared. I fight to win. If I attack now, I will lead my men into defeat.' Indira Gandhi was aghast at the affront by the General. Manekshaw went on, 'If I attack now, the mountain passes in the North-East Frontier are free of snow and China may attack. The rivers in Bangladesh turn into an ocean with the onset of monsoons, making invasion impossible. Out of my 181 tanks, only eleven are battleworthy. I have to move the ordinance and equipment and fuel and food and ammunition and troops and allied support services to the borders. The IAF and Navy will not be ready to support the attack. I need six months. I will be ready to attack in December. Prime Minister, now give me your orders.'

When he was summoned to her office again that evening, Manekshaw had carried his resignation paper in his pocket and asked her as he went in, 'Do you want my resignation?' Indira Gandhi said, 'No, because everything you tell me is true.' The rest is history.

When the head of a country calls a cabinet meeting along with the cabinet secretary and other top officials of the government, like the NSA, the head of disaster management, the home secretary, etc., to discuss any momentous decision in the offing, we need people to stand up and speak truth to power. In the present case, they should have advised the Prime Minister that a meeting with all the chief ministers, followed by meetings with chief secretaries and heads of police in the states, were necessary before announcing the lockdown to not only obtain their cooperation but also to get their feedback, which would have helped evolve a well-thought-out plan on how to implement the lockdown and decide on all aspects of the minimum lifeline of logistics and supply chains.

The political leader may have a larger objective, a daring mission and an overarching vision that others may lack, but let us bear in mind that the head of any country cannot be expected to possess all the knowledge or ability himself to anticipate the fall-out of such measures. The right answers and solutions will always emerge as we have no dearth of capable and knowledgeable people in the government and the country. What we lack are courageous leaders and professionals in the bureaucracy, the police and the military, who can speak truth to power.

*Deccan Herald*, April 2020

# Book for a Book, not Bullets

In a flash, in a moment of senseless madness, a life was snuffed out three years ago on 5 September. A luminous mind extinguished. A lithe, vibrant, sylph-like woman cut down by a hail of bullets by assailants with links to 'Hindu right-wing' groups who are now in jail but yet to face trial. Gauri Lankesh was irrepressible and irreverent. Fired with a crusading zeal, she challenged and confronted right-wing bigots and zealots, often fighting for the poor and the marginalized. She took up cudgels on behalf of the Naxals, and she lionized left-leaning student leaders like Kanhaiya Kumar. She was not a card-carrying communist, but a fire-breathing socialist, rationalist and journalist-activist. That was her public persona. In private, she was caring, humane and loving.

Initially, it appeared the attack was carried out by unknown contract killers. With public pressure mounting, Karnataka police finally succeeded in cracking the case, arresting many individuals radicalized by fringe Hindu outfits who are alleged to have murdered Gauri. The police investigation connected the dots to a common link to the murders of Gauri and other well-known academics and rationalists who were gunned down earlier – the Vice-Chancellor of

Gulbarga University in Karnataka's M.M. Kalburgi and Narendra Dabholkar and Govind Pansare in Maharashtra.

The investigations ultimately led through intricate back alleys and a convoluted network of shadow cells to the apex of a right-wing Hindutva organization that was silencing mainly left-leaning intellectuals and rationalists who were Hindus. Girish Karnad and U.R. Ananthamurthy were also on their 'hit list' of people who were fighting against fundamentalism and superstition and injustice against Dalits. A question is often asked by Hindu fundamentalists (an oxymoron, as they are not true Hindus), 'Why do leftists attack only Hindus? Do they dare to attack believers of Islam or other religions?' But does that give anyone the right to kill those of their own religion or of other faiths who question the many ills, like untouchability, that plague Hindu society?

Bertrand Russell said, 'I would never die for my beliefs, because I could be wrong.' By the same token, you cannot kill someone for their beliefs, because you could be mistaken. By the same logic, it follows that you could be murdered for your beliefs, too. If 'pseudo-secularists' can be killed, then 'pseudo-Hindutva' proponents can also be slain. Life is not possible with such a twisted dialectic. If we all aspire to live in a democratic, egalitarian and free society, we must resolve our differences through dialogue.

Gauri Lankesh held extreme views. True. Her language was not always sober. It was often aggressive, provocative even, and at times needlessly strident while exposing others. It could have been tempered, more civil and sensitive. So is the language of Muslim and Hindu hardliners and many leaders on either side of the social and political divide. Does that give anyone a licence to kill them as their views are abhorrent?

Gauri supported the demands of Lingayats to declare their sect as a separate religion, and that raised the hackles of many Hindu right-wing leaders and outfits. Hinduism has faced such challenges before. It has always had the strength and resilience to absorb and digest the heretics, rebels, agnostics and atheists and invading faiths like a boa constrictor, as Octavio Paz said, and accommodate them in its fold and celebrate the diversity with its rich and varied polytheism.

Gauri was seen as being prejudiced against the right-wing while turning a blind eye to the atrocities and violence perpetrated by the leftists, or the killings of RSS workers in Kerala by the left-led alliance or the murder of innocents by the Naxals. But none of that can justify the taking of her life. That deed, done in the name of protecting Hinduism, will be a blot on the love, tolerance and non-violence that Hinduism stands for.

The leaders of the Hindu community, from across its numerous religious orders and outfits, must come out and strongly condemn any violence or killing and speak out against the poison of intolerance. They must courageously speak up against khap panchayats and cow vigilantes. Similarly, the Muslim leadership – both the clerics and the community's intellectuals and political leaders across the spectrum – should come forth and denounce the killings by Islamic terror outfits. They must speak up against their religious laws that are incompatible with a modern, democratic society. A few on both sides have done so, but many have been silent or equivocal. They have to take a clear stand, so that no one is in the slightest doubt about whether they are on the side of a humane, pluralistic society that is open and free or if they wish to stand alongside bigots and fanatics who are ready to kill those who have a different worldview. Silence is not an option.

An unbeliever himself, Albert Camus, on being invited to address Christians of the Dominican Monastery in 1948, spoke passionately: 'The grouping we need is a grouping of men resolved to speak out clearly and to pay up personally ... what I feel like telling you today is that the world needs real dialogue, that falsehood is just as much the opposite of dialogue as silence, and that the only possible dialogue is the kind between people who remain what they are and speak their minds. When a Spanish bishop blesses political executions, he ceases to be a bishop or a Christian or even a man; he is a dog just like one who, backed by an ideology, orders that execution without doing the dirty work himself ... In that case, Christians will live and

Christianity will die.' That warning applies to all of us of the various religions today.

It is well to remember what former Prime Minister Atal Behari Vajpayee said: 'Kitaab ka jawaab kitaab se hota hai.' A book (argument) must be answered by books (arguments), not bullets.

*Deccan Herald*, September 2020

# Encounter Killings: When Truth Is Forever Banished to the Realm of Conjecture

I was having lunch with a retired Karnataka director general of police (DGP) on that Thursday afternoon. He had at one time headed prisons and also had a stint in the Intelligence Bureau (IB), so was serving up some macabre stories from the days when he headed one of the largest prisons of Bangalore, which held 5,000 prisoners. For dessert, we scooped up a few heart-warming stories about hardened criminals. That was when the news broke: Vikas Dubey had surrendered at an Ujjain temple. We exchanged knowing glances. The police chief finally broke his silence. 'It will be the stupidest thing for the police to kill him. But that will likely be his fate. In fact, protecting him from rivals or even allies who may want him exterminated and ensuring he doesn't take his own life should be their utmost priority … so that they can investigate his modus operandi, his infrastructure, his informants, his nexus of politicians, bureaucrats and business associates, his money trail and so forth.' Barely eighteen hours later, there was another flash: Dubey had been killed. It strains credulity that a dreaded criminal who surrenders voluntarily, unarmed, will try to escape right after, grabbing a weapon from a policeman's holster. The truth here is forever banished to the realm of conjecture. But what will stay even beyond the reach of that are the facts behind Dubey's network: the powerful people under whose patronage he prospered, without whose help he could not have ambushed and killed eight policemen.

## Logic is a fugitive

Among the many memories that this dredged up, top of the pile is the still-vivid one of the Andhra Pradesh cops killing all four accused in the Hyderabad gangrape–murder last year. The similarities are striking. At an obvious level, the *mise en scene* itself. The Hyderabad cops, incredibly, led the accused to the scene of the crime at three in the morning without handcuffs. Now, the UP cops were transporting Dubey in a police van without securing him. The script thereafter seems so well-rehearsed that any kid could enact it blindfolded – an attempted break for freedom, and bullets shot from the back that often miraculously pierce the chest. So much for method and circumstances. The real underlying continuity, however, is psychological. It relates to the public validation, the sense of justice being done. Indeed, even relief. People feel this is swift and well-deserved retribution for brutal, sadistic criminals. Sure enough, social media was full of praise for the police both times. A blood-curdling, gory and unspeakable crime had been avenged.

Yes, like now, many had questioned the veracity of the government version then too. Among the sceptics were many distinguished retired police officers. Even in the Dubey case, one of the wives of the cops who lost his life in the ambush laid by the gangster said, 'I feel happy Dubey paid the price, but how can you now investigate his nexus with people in power?' The sceptics mince no words: many civil society activists, lawyers, journalists and retired senior cops allege it was a stage-managed extrajudicial killing. Twitter is on fire with a flood of sceptical comments and jibes. Journalist Ravi Nair asked, 'Why should a criminal who surrendered to the police try to escape? The story of Bal Narendra catching a crocodile is more believable.'

## The birth of vigilantism

And yet, when I read the news, I heard myself saying 'Thank God'. I was startled at my own reaction. There was a ghost lurking inside me too, a vigilante craving for the swift avenging of injustice! The sheer horror of the cruelty inflicted on the innocent girl in Hyderabad, the way her life was so wantonly extinguished, the inconsolable widows and children of the eight cops, the way they wept at the funeral ... all this had shaken me to the core too, like everyone else. And the consequence, I could now see, was the rage rising in me presently. Though deeply aware that a crime cannot justify another crime, I found myself almost imperceptibly drawn to the edge, and couldn't help feeling a sense of shame... and wonder.

What brings this about? Not too difficult to tease out this strand, really. After all, who has not cheered lustily when a John Wayne or a Rajnikant pummels his fists into the face of the villain, or when Clint Eastwood sprays bullets into the knees of the 'Bad' Lee Van Cleef or digs his cowboy boots with spurs right into evil's face? In *Sholay*, when an enraged Dharmendra beats the ultimate villain into pulp and is about to kill him, Thakur stops him: he has a spiked boot with which to dispense justice himself. A justice that's inextricably bound up with revenge: coming from a retired policeman, this was vigilante justice at its best. The popular literary traditions of both the West and East are embellished with vigilante heroes and stories of outlaws who do good. Always, the system itself is cruel, and you must step outside it to be good, to do good. It is the staple of Indian cinema, in every language. Every road in our popular culture leads to that kerbside in Kanpur where jeeps overturn mysteriously, almost by the force of public will.

## Dexter checks in

Something about the jubilation of the crowds, the showering of petals on Hyderabad's shooter cops and the open justifications issued by older 'encounter' heroes reminds me of the popular Netflix show *Dexter*. Dexter Morgan a forensic blood spatter analyst with the Miami Police, is an orphan whose mother was murdered with a chainsaw by drug dealers. He grew up as an adopted child of a police officer. The double helix of revenge and the law is already formed. Dexter is a man possessed, on a mission to bring the most inhuman serial rapists and killers to justice. But sure enough, the apparatus of justice is weak, and the baddies nearly always get to roam free again. No surprises from here on: he becomes a self-styled vigilante, egged on and counselled by his foster daddy. Blood samples and DNA tests offer a modicum of method, a self-validating trail towards extra-legal justice. Once having convinced himself of someone's guilt, he executes them with cool, clinical efficiency and disposes of the body parts in the ocean. Dexter is an affable cop, a loveable hero, a normal guy with a nice girlfriend, a Robin Hood with a pleasing Yankee twang – you can't help taking a liking to him. He caters to that deeply embedded demon in all of us, the one who wants the villain punished in this life. I found myself waiting with bated breath, almost desperate for Dexter to catch and execute the rapist-killer every time I watched the show.

## A spreading blood stain

A smooth transition is offered to us – the cop as the nice guy, just like we like to imagine ourselves to be, one who's moved by injustice and yet helpless because the justice system of which he's a part doesn't deliver justice. So the criminal must be made to bleed outside the system. But it is never that simple. It is actually injustice that bleeds across the spectrum. It is crime that spreads. When a cop's blood is on the hands of the gangster, the way they gang up and pursue him till he's extinguished is right out of the feudal vendetta playbook – an honour killing. 'Vigilantes often justify their actions as a fulfilment of the wishes of the community,' say studies. But 'the wishes of the community' are not necessarily driven snow. The patterns of social violence should be enough to make us vigilant about self-validating referrals to the community as the third umpire. It is true that politicians when in power, are loath to create robust, independent institutions. The answer can only be to bring enough pressure on them to act, not to have that vacuum suck up all ethics in the rest of the landscape too. A grey world where we are resigned to the fact that the Hyderabad case may take a decade in the courts. Where Dubey will become a file, or perhaps a Netflix series. To midwife the eternal rebirth of vigilantism in the public mind.

## Best medicine for vigilante violence

What we need is for the instruments of justice to fill the void. It is about time institutions like the police and CBI are made truly independent of ruling parties. The BJP does not seem to be keen on this, nor the regional parties. And the Congress did little on this front during its long rule since Independence. We must force their hand collectively. And most urgently, we must audit our own emotions. Take Unnao, Nirbhaya, Hyderabad, the recent Tuticorin custodial deaths and now the Dubey killing: we may be tempted to say, like John Bunyan in his novel, 'Hanging is too good for him.' But we must beware. Howsoever cruel the crime, vigilante justice only leads to more abomination. A hazy trail transports us from there to the world of wanton lynching, cow vigilantism or mob killings on hearsay or driven by religious passions. The line between ordinary crime and mass social violence is pretty thin. Once the idea is instituted that the public will deliver justice, it doesn't stop at uniformed Rambos taking down a few baddies. While fighting monsters, we ourselves become monsters. There is also the minor issue of innocence. Sometimes culpability is clear, sometimes not – even in a crime. In society, there are only innocents. As the retired police boss left my house, a shadow of sadness hovered on his face.

*Outlook*, July 2020

# Kerala – No Country for Young Women

From what I can remember of my grandmother, only one image of her comes to my mind – of a widow with a tonsured head, wrapped on top in a dull brown cotton saree worn in the traditional style, a blank forehead without the usual red vermilion or kumkum, bare neck, empty ears and hands unadorned and shorn of all jewellery. Her ankles and feet were bare, too, without the traditional anklets or silver rings worn on the toes of both feet – the symbol of married women.

A very vivid story of my grandmother is etched in my memory. I had gone to Melkote, the idyllic temple town near Mysore – where she lived with one of her sons, my maternal uncle – during my school summer holidays from Gorur, where I studied in the local government Kannada medium school.

In those days, a favourite vacation was being taken to your mother's birthplace to be with your grandmother, carefree and pampered. I must have been eight or nine. My older sister was by my side. I'm not sure what triggered this poignant episode that my grandmother recounted, but it was heart-rending. Her eyes had welled up, and with dreamy eyes staring into her distant past she narrated this event.

She was married off as a child bride of thirteen to a boy – also young, just sixteen – who was studying to be a Sanskrit pundit and training to become a purohit (priest) in Melkote, a Srivaishnavite pilgrim centre founded by Ramanuja a thousand years ago. When she was in her late thirties, her husband took ill and died. She had three children – two boys and a girl, my mother. They were all in their teens and in school.

She was in total shock and grief. But what she remembered with unbearable pain was the day the various ceremonies and rituals were performed in public in the presence of relatives and other locals of the village, the manner in which her widowhood was formalized and announced. She was seated on the floor amidst two priests, who, surrounded by many relatives, chanted various mantras.

First, they removed all her ornaments, including her mangalasutra – the holy necklace that her husband had tied around her neck on the day of her wedding. Then they smashed the glass bangles on her wrists contemptuously, removed the rings in her ear lobes and her toes, unfastened the anklets and erased her vermilion roughly even as she shook and sobbed inconsolably, drowning in her sorrow.

A village barber, who was ready and waiting with his sharpened blades, was ushered in to perform the ritual of tonsuring her head. As she was bent, broken in sorrow, the barber shaved her head, and she recalled with tears how her copious and luxuriant tresses fell to the ground. The chanting continued. She was dizzy and overwhelmed by the events. Then she was led to the bath, and after her relatives poured water on her and scrubbed her, she was given a plain brown cotton saree, which became her prison uniform for the rest of her life.

The message was clear and writ large. She was now branded a widow. She was deliberately disfigured, made over to look ugly, divested of all her finery and jewels and condemned to live an austere life in a corner permanently with a tonsured head, to be shaven twice a month. It was to ensure that she would never be attractive to draw the attention of men.

That story and those soul-piercing images still haunt me when I think of her. And images of other widows that I occasionally saw in many homes float before my eyes as I think about the cruelty and horror they must have endured when their husbands died.

Thankfully, such abominable rituals and barbaric practices – a curse from the Vedic past – are rare these days, but discrimination against widows and their ill-treatment is still prevalent in many parts of India. Widow remarriage is no longer uncommon. Untouchability is still practised in devious ways but assertion, affirmative action and empowerment of Dalits and stringent punishment guaranteed under the law are good deterrents.

Child marriage and the practice of sati are all things of the past fortunately, thanks to visionary and courageous reformers like Raja Ram Mohan Roy and others. Many young people today can never believe that such terrible and inhuman practices existed not too long ago.

When you pause and consider the foregoing, you are shocked at the reactions of many fire-breathing fanatics, frothing at the mouth on television panel discussions, hysterically protesting against the entry of women of the menstruating age (arbitrarily decided as ages ten to fifty) into the Sabarimala temple – even after the recent Supreme Court verdict allowing women of all ages entry into the sanctum sanctorum of the temple to end any kind of gender discrimination against women.

The Supreme Court judgement was in line with the spirit and broader tenets of the Constitution when it passed many recent landmark judgements – notably against triple talaq, criminalization of homosexuals, discrimination of LGBTQs and a few others. The hypocrisy of both the Congress and the BJP stands out and is laughable and shameful.

The Congress, a party that presents itself as progressive and liberal while painting the BJP as communal, has no qualms in blissfully opposing triple talaq – all for the sake of Muslim votes, just as it opposed the historic Shah Bano judgement when Rajiv Gandhi was the Prime Minister by amending the law.

The BJP is hell-bent on enforcing the triple talaq law to consolidate a Hindu-majority vote bank by portraying itself as anti-Islamic. In Sabarimala, the BJP lawmakers – though in the ruling party – are making a laughing stock of themselves, without even a pretence of concern to uphold the Constitution. The party is brazenly defying and disregarding the Supreme Court verdict, offering warped logic in justifying the ban on entry of women into the Sabarimala temple while in the same breath welcoming the triple talaq judgement.

What is good for the goose is not good for the gander. Different strokes for different religions. While the BJP is displaying a reformist zeal to liberate Muslim women, it has no hesitation to trample on the rights and dignity of Hindu women. Endorsing khap panchayats, imposing medieval dress codes or banning entry of women to temples are all attempts to create a feudal society along the lines of an Islamic State.

The Congress Party's actions are as regressive, perched on two blinkered horses, both on a gallop – one trying to outdo the Muslims by supporting triple talaq to ingratiate itself into their demographic, and the other trying to appease the Hindu vote bank by upholding primitive traditions that are a blot on a civilized society.

Hindu women all over India do not generally visit any public temples during menstruation, voluntarily avoiding it even where there are no bans of any kind. They do not even light lamps before deities or offer any prayers, even in their own homes. It is a self-imposed restriction based on their personal beliefs. It is voluntary, and there is no policing. It is discreet and dignified. But imposing a ban by male priests in a public place of worship on women who are of the menstruating age is medieval, discriminating and humiliating.

Decades hence when we look back at the Sabarimala incidents, they will hopefully be part of our shameful past – consigned to the dustbins of history – and our grandchildren will look at them incredulously, just as they now think of sati or tonsuring of widows.

*The Wire*, January 2019

# POLITICS

# India – Betwixt and Between – Neither an Authoritarian State Nor a Liberal Democracy

India seems betwixt and between – neither an authoritarian state nor a democracy, neither a developed economy nor a backward country. It has made great scientific strides, but many of its people and political leaders are also under the spell of ancient myths of our past glory and are lost in age-old superstitions. It is neither a totalitarian Hindu state nor an enlightened democracy with secular credentials, neither ruled by a dictator nor governed by a liberal democrat. India and the idea of India are neither fully one thing nor properly the other. It has always been an enigma.

Though the international reports downgrading India on many parameters that determine a vibrant democracy may not be entirely accurate, the perception of India, a beacon until now for the rest of the world, is in danger of becoming a diminishing democracy. Perceptions matter. Is Modi a tyrant comparable to the dictators of the past, a Stalin of the former Union of Soviet Socialist Republics (USSR), a Hitler of Germany, who put millions to death? Or can he be likened to modern-day despots – Putin of Russia, Erdogan of

Turkey, Mohammed Bin Salman, the present de facto ruler of Saudi Arabia or Xi Jinping of China – some of whom have not hesitated to ruthlessly eliminate their opponents through blood-curdling methods or simply made them disappear overnight without a trace? Such comparisons may be far-fetched. His fiercest and most bitter high profile critics – political leaders and intellectuals – are roaming free, attacking him at will and critiquing him copiously. Can you imagine a Rahul Gandhi, Mamata Banerjee, Pratap Bhanu Mehta or Ram Guha walking free in China or Russia after criticizing those governments? But does that make Modi a liberal democrat? No one may give him that certificate. For every Ram Guha or P.B. Mehta, there are scores of Sudha Bhardwajs and Teltumbdes languishing in jail without a fair and speedy trial. His millions of fans who see him as a demigod would approve of many of his autocratic ways. The country was adrift; his predecessor was weak. A messiah was needed, and Modi was sent.

Modi is thoroughly modern but also worships false gods – he pushes for solar energy and vaccines and Rafale fighter jets but also invokes cosmic energy to drive out the coronavirus by exhorting the public to beat gongs and conches at auspicious hours based on ancient numerology. He praises India as the largest vaccine producer in the world but does not pull up his cabinet colleagues when they launch voodoo medicines of a Baba to fight the coronavirus, a drug that has no clinical evidence of trials and condemned by the Indian Medical Association. He is, in a sense, like the countless Indians who embrace modernity without abandoning their obscurantist superstitions.

Modi is not the despot that many Indian intellectuals compare him to, but his devotees may not be able to effectively parry the charges of many of his authoritarian ways. His fiery oratory – be it on the Rama temple, beef ban, protection of the holy cow, his party's narrow definition of nationalism, intolerance to criticism, the Citizenship Amendment Act (CAA) and status of migrants – and his espousal of a brazen majoritarian politics may have encouraged vigilante justice, resulting in the killing through lynching of innocent people among minority communities. His silence at times and reluctance to rein in his overzealous officials and the rabid elements of his party could have resulted in the incarceration of numerous dissenting academics, critical journalists and protesting students and could have triggered violence between various sections of society. It is alleged that his penchant for reforms by ramming them through executive orders and ordinances without consultations, even if well-intended, may have brought miseries on his people.

Even so, is India an authoritarian state? Are its people happy? Are they free?

Sweden's V-Dem Institute, which publishes an annual Democracy report, described India as an electoral autocracy in its 2021 report. If it were true that many of India's formal institutions are compromised, including the election machinery, and the democracy totally undermined and the media suppressed, Delhi wouldn't have been ruled by Arvind Kejriwal, Punjab by Amarinder Singh, Andhra by Jagan Reddy, who is a Christian, and Telangana by K. Chandrashekhar Rao. Almost 70 per cent of India constitutes non-BJP states. In the just-concluded local civic body elections in Andhra Pradesh, Jagan Reddy's Congress completely wiped out the BJP. Yet there are elements of truth in the report.

Washington's Freedom House Index has rated India as partly free as a democracy and placed it in the same bracket as Pakistan. The United Nations' World Happiness Report 2020 places India at the 139th position out of 149 countries featured and has ranked India below these countries: Libya (80th), Belarus (75th), Venezuela (107th), Niger (96th), Pakistan (105th), Saudi Arabia (21st).

So when an international research body positions India way below Saudi Arabia, for example, where a dissenting journalist, a Saudi national, can be dismembered by an execution squad and dissolved in acids and where people are beheaded in full public view for violation of Islamic laws and an adulteress can be stoned to death, you are in disbelief that Indians are the least happy in the world and you would wish to trash the research reports. Findings and generalizations born out of statistics can often distort reality. If a man were to hold a red-hot iron rod in his left hand and ice in his right hand, he would be scalded on one and suffer frostbite on the other. But a statistician would say his mean body temperature is nice and warm.

And yet, it will be imprudent to ignore these reports. Many strong leaders easily fall into what Bertrand Russell called 'The Administrator's Fallacy'. He pointed out that they are liable to imagine that the state they administer is a tidy and neat organism and homogenous. And they wish to fit men to systems rather than systems to men. Human beings and their communities are infinitely complex and diverse with their desires, traits and proclivities. Diversity, creativity, freedom and liberty are the necessary conditions for progress and happiness and the flowering of democracy and civilization.

India is at a crossroads. Where must India head now? Should Modi be guided by his jingoistic advisors, who are advocating a policy of isolation and misplaced muscular nationalism and practice of politics and governance that favours one community over another, not to mention inward-looking self-reliance bordering on hubris? That path may lead India into a 'climate of intellectual incest', as Arthur Koestler said, and stunt its growth from 'ever-widening thought and action', leaving a nation 'fragmented by narrow domestic walls'.

On the contrary, should he pursue building a genuine democracy that will enable a healthy milieu of economic, political, social and cultural worlds that encompasses and nourishes our rich diversity of languages, literature, music and the arts that will lead to a happy and egalitarian society? We can be reminded of a line from the *Rigveda*: 'Let noble thoughts come to us from every side.'

India can be a leading light in the comity of nations by following the latter path, and Modi, with his mandate and stature, is well placed to lead India to that exalted position.

If he did so, it could be his lasting legacy.

*The Times of India*, April 2021

# Salami Slicing Chinese Style

There are calls for the economic boycott of China. Politicians are throwing muck at each other. Diplomats are calling for caution and shrewd diplomacy, whatever it may mean. But when the enemy has breached the palace gates, you first fight them tooth and nail and repulse them before any other considerations.

Politicians generally act and speak with their eyes on their vote bank or the next elections, often fighting imaginary demons. 'The whole aim of practical politics is to keep the populace alarmed (and hence clamorous to be led to safety) by menacing it with an endless series of hobgoblins, all of them imaginary,' said H.L. Mencken. The recent Chinese Dragon Dance on the icy heights of Ladakh's Galwan valley was not an imaginary Chinese opera of goblins but a menacing dance of death that left twenty Indian soldiers, including their commanding officer, dead and unknown casualties on the Chinese side. The Chinese are cocking a snook at India and have entrenched themselves across the LAC. These were failures of foresight and intelligence, possibly a result of hubris or naïveté by our leadership. Politicians of both sides, though they may now be trying to take political advantage of the border clash, accusing and discrediting one another (the Congress blaming Modi for appeasing the Chinese and not standing up to Xi Jinping, whom he went out of the way to woo and placate, and the BJP once again exhuming the ghosts of Nehru and his dynasty for all of India's problems, including China), it must be emphasized that none of our politicians, including those in the Opposition, are enemies of the state, though they are undermining India's interests by their partisan ways. The ruling party should take all parties into confidence and deal with China unitedly, and everyone must put aside temptations of scoring political points to be able to effectively deal with Chinese aggression.

If party politics and personality-driven diplomacy (Nehru too was carried away by his personal rapport with Zhou En Lai and his charm) can be put aside and tackled institutionally while dealing with China, a country that is a big trading partner and now a sizeable investor, which has albeit turned belligerent militarily and is trying to slice off parts of Indian territory like salami in what Chief Minister Capt. Amarinder Singh, a soldier himself, termed 'the salami slicing policy', appropriating border areas over the years by nibbling away here and there, then it will make it easier to deal with a bullying neighbour who has breached the gates. The first rule is that India must not mix economics, diplomacy and military tactics when under military attack. Though they all ultimately have a bearing on each other, they must be critically analysed separately on their own merits.

There are strident calls now with affected rage and theatrics – burning effigies of Xi Jinping, comically torching even wrong effigies of Kim Jong-un of North Korea – to boycott Chinese goods. Many are clamouring for a ban on new Chinese investments and even demanding cancellation of contracts already signed. That will be cutting off one's nose to spite one's face. Instead, China must be given a bloody nose militarily. Though the companies are Chinese, the investments are in India and will hurt millions of Indians who are employed in these companies and will have an adverse ripple effect on various sectors of the economy, including banking. India's trade issues and investment policies must be viewed independent of border skirmishes, taking a matured, long-term view, and evolved by our economists and experts in commerce and trade and negotiated skilfully and astutely to a mutually rewarding and sustainable partnership. And this is always a work in progress. It is important to send a clear message to the Chinese investors that while India will not renege on its investments and trade policies, their military transgressions will be met militarily. That will in turn put pressure on the Chinese rulers to keep their constituency back home happy. This will also reinforce confidence among global investors that India will show prudence and not react emotionally in a knee-jerk manner. The late fiery trade union leader George Fernandes, after the Emergency, in 1977, when he became a union minister for industries after winning the parliament election, in a fit of rage ordered American multinationals IBM and Coca-Cola to leave the country unceremoniously. This hurt India more than the United States. We cannot commit such errors in the heat of the moment. On the contrary, this will give better leverage to India while negotiating with China, which will be lost if they are kicked out altogether. And there will also be retaliation on Indians working in China and Indian exports to China. Of course there can be deterrents against new investments, but in the globalized economy we are inextricably linked to many countries, and in the case of China, there is already a huge trade surplus vis-à-vis India that has widened disproportionately due to the policies of successive governments, more so during this regime. And trade imbalance must be bridged by astute economic policies and reforms by India gaining ground in some areas that give it advantage over China, instead of policies remaining mere slogans.

In matters of geopolitics, the present leadership will do well to consult respected former diplomats and defence analysts and retired generals who have advised previous governments on security and geopolitics with China. This will help the present team advising the Prime Minister to gain insight into the adversary's mind and counter it and evolve sound pre-emptive policies. We have many highly regarded apolitical and bipartisan professionals – defence analysts, ambassadors, former service chiefs from the Army, Navy and Air

Force – who have dealt with China in various capacities with earlier governments. They must be brought to the table for, after all, over the years, these professionals will have learnt from their mistakes of misreading a cunning adversary and their experience will help you know your enemy. What better axiom than the one from the great Chinese general and revered philosopher Sun Tzu:

> 'If you know the enemy and know yourself, you need not fear the result of a hundred battles. If you know yourself but not the enemy, for every victory gained you will also suffer a defeat. If you know neither the enemy nor yourself, you will succumb in every battle.'

Prudent diplomatic and geopolitical policies on the one hand and build-up of military capabilities and related strategy and tactics on the other have to be pursued together, aided by strategic intelligence. But when deliberate enemy incursions, encroachments to build camps and entrenchments or attacks on our soldiers inside our territory take place, then they have to be met with instant and heavy retaliation. An enemy attack should never be answered by diplomatic backlash, tepid dialogues, economic retaliation or blockade, though these can continue in the back alleys. A military assault has to be met militarily every time. No quarter whatever be given to an enemy to kill with impunity or invade and occupy and present a fait accompli. In fact, for dialogues and diplomacy and peace initiatives to be successful, the enemy must know they cannot get an inch of land by stealthy or brazen incursions unless they are ready to risk very heavy casualties themselves.

Never appease a bully. It will only embolden them.

*The Times of India*, June 2020

# Is Our Paradise Lost?

This is not about politicians or their parties. Politicians come and go. You only have to look back at the recent events in Maharashtra. The fanatic rushed and tied the knot with the secular. They abandon their gods and change their ideologies as easily as they change their saffron robes and white caps and hop into each other's beds. This is about nostalgia, about our hearts and their longing for the joy and bonhomie and togetherness that seem elusive today. There was a time, until not long ago, when despite all our travails and tribulations and sorrows and strife, our land seemed 'apparelled in celestial light'. Can we regain that paradise?

Let me recount a short story. My village, picturesque Gorur, lies on the bank of the river Hemavati, a tributary of the Cauvery. Like many villages of rural old Mysore, it is a composite village comprising of many castes – carpenters, blacksmiths, fishermen, barbers, potters, weavers and others – but the Harijan, as always, lived in a satellite colony outside the village, a blemish from our ancient past, a stain no amount of chanting of mantras and bathing in the holy river can wash clean.

The Harijans ate beef, like the Muslims. They carried the dead cows from the village, skinned them and stripped them of all flesh and took them to the local Muslim, who cured the leather and sent it to the tannery and crushed the bones and sent those to the factory. The village and its people lived in perfect symbiosis and happy harmony. But it was easy to see that the Harijans had a special kinship with the Muslims; their life was more entwined with the latter, unlike the uneasy, unequal relationship with the Hindu community.

Aji Saheb, the Muslim who purchased the cattle skin and bones from the Dalits in our village, was also a rice merchant. I remember vividly that he often came home to buy harvested paddy. A big man who sported a huge white kurta and baggy pyjamas, he was highly regarded for his ethical business dealings, was amiable and had a good sense of humour, poking fun at Brahmins and their orthodox and austere lifestyle. And my father and uncles would chaff and laugh.

His father was nicknamed 'Shawl Saheb'. In a famous eponymous story by Gorur Ramaswamy Iyengar, he narrates an incident. Once, Iyengar's father, a priest, was in deep meditation and chanting mantras in the back garden of his house. Aji Saheb's father, not very well-to-do, came home to meet him just then and sat down on a stone bench opposite the priest. As the chanting went on interminably, Saheb Senior spied a lovely, embroidered shawl on the tulasi katte. It was monsoon – it was raining heavily, and there was a chill in the air. Saheb Senior, emboldened by the knowledge that the priest wouldn't open his eyes while in deep meditation, picked up the shawl, wrapped himself up cosily and walked out confidently even as the priest's wife watched dumbfounded. Next day, when Saheb Senior came, brazenly wearing the same shawl, the priest – my great grandfather – asked him why he hadn't at least asked him before taking it. Saheb Senior replied nonchalantly that it was cold and he needed the shawl, but he was too scared to disturb a Brahmin in prayer and incur his wrath!

My father would often remind Aji Saheb of this story and demand that the shawl be returned, and both of them would break into hearty laughter.

Ah, how far we have come from that idyll, from that simplicity of rural identities and from the lost world I'm homesick about. We all have such stories and reminiscences. The villages still preserve much of the past, but the urban centres are becoming cesspools of hatred, overcome by senseless violence and festering wounds, with an uneasy calm between communities. We are unthinkingly lapping up false narratives and distorted histories that are woven and fed to us about Muslim kings and Hindu kings. Many Hindu kings had Muslim commanders and vice versa. Hindu kings allied with Muslim kings to defeat other Hindu chieftains or Muslim rulers. Shivaji's father Shahaji captured Bangalore from Kempegowda II by allying himself with the ruler of Bijapur Ranadulla Khan. It was common. Girish Karnad's historical plays explored existential issues of intrigue, power play and despair of those times, and blended the past with the present to make it relevant to our times. As Karnad said with reference to his last play, *Rakshasa Tangadi*, which captured the details of a battle and its machinations during the rule of Aliya Rama Raya of the Vijayanagar Empire, it was to dispel the 'mainstream narrative that whitewashed it as Hindu–Muslim conflict'.

Why has our urban, smug, consuming middle class become so gross? Why do they feed themselves on hatred? They do not love, do not read, listen to good music or lose themselves in nature, which ennobles and uplifts. They gorge on television news and social media in all waking hours. Can our civilization flower when fire-breathing mullahs sympathize with jihadis who murder, and the Trishul-wielding Hindu justifies killing through lynching? If we scorn all faiths but appease one faith at the expense of another or embrace a moribund ideology and justify violence or abandon all the cherished ideals of our scriptures and teachings of Meera and Kabir, and Ghalib and Gandhi, can our children blossom in such a feuding land? Can we be true Christians or Muslims or true Vaishnavs if we hate and hurt another soul, as the fifteenth-century Gujarati Saint Narsi Mehta sang in '*Vaishnava Janato*', Gandhi's favourite hymn?

Can we reclaim that lost paradise where we heard the soul-stirring shehnai of Ustad Bismillah Khan in Kashi Viswanath Temple, Pandit

Jasraj singing '*Allah ho meherban*' after singing '*Bhagavate Hey Vasudeva*' at the Ram Navami festival in full-throated ease, Bade Ghulam Ali Khan rendering a glorious '*Hari Om Tat Sat*' bhajan or M.S. Subbulakshmi singing a Kabir song followed by a Meera bhajan with equal aplomb and devotion?

Can we prosper by 'returning to our ghosts and demons which reason had exorcised?' Our faiths, whatever they be, must be to an overarching fealty to love, to fraternity and solidarity and to all creation under an abode of comingling faiths so that we rejoice together, as in our former days.

As Tagore said, 'While God waits for his temple to be built of love, men bring stones.' And we are busy building barriers.

*Deccan Herald*, May 2020

# When Governments Play Peeping Tom: Why India Should Be Worried About the Pegasus Row

Legend has it that Thomas the tailor got the sobriquet 'Peeping Tom' because he peeped through his window to watch Lady Godiva riding naked on her horse through the streets of Coventry in England and was struck blind. It is a different matter that Godiva, the wife of a nobleman, was naive enough to expect everyone not to follow their primaeval urge to ogle at her when she announced she would be trotting across the street on her steed nude, covered only by her tresses, and ordered everyone to shut their doors and windows and stay indoors.

Voyeurism, peeping through keyholes, prying through bedroom windows, secretly watching others in sexual acts or, more generally, watching other people's private lives is not uncommon and exists only among the human species. But eavesdropping, phone- and wire-tapping, planting bugs, snooping and spying have been prevalent for ages among kings, commoners, governments, police and intelligence agencies.

Film lore and novels – from *Sherlock Holmes* to *James Bond* – are full of it. Only the modus operandi changes and is often influenced by changes in technology.

English model Christine Keeler slept with both the Russian naval attaché Yevgeny Ivanov and British Secretary of State for War John Profumo during the height of the Cold War and had pillow talks with the lover to whose country she owed higher allegiance. President John F. Kennedy had an extra-marital relationship with Judith Exner, who was also having an affair with mobster Sam Giancana, the Chicago Godfather, which compromised the presidency.

Satellites are also extensively used to spy on countries and zero-in on terrorists using sophisticated high-end imaging cameras and listening devices. The ancient method of the so-called honey trap may still be more effective in seducing the head of a state to steal secrets than the use of the most advanced gadgets. All this, however, is passé.

## New-age snooping

Enter Israeli cyber firm NSO which uses a spyware software named Pegasus. It has added a whole new dimension to snooping and spying. Unlike phone tapping, bugging, wireless eavesdropping or snooping through hidden micro-cameras or other devices, Pegasus completely hijacks and takes over the targeted individual's smartphone. Your WhatsApp messages, emails, cameras, video and voice calls, location, etc., are all compromised. The spyware can insert fake mails and content to incriminate, frame and blackmail the target, according to media reports.

Imagine having an invisible person tagging along to your bedroom, washroom, drawing room and also accompanying you to the office, conference room as well as hitching a ride in your car. And they can move your stuff or put new things in your bedroom or the office, unbeknown to you. In short, they can wreck your life.

Pegasus is in the eye of a storm and stands exposed globally. NSO's website says it offers its spyware only as a tool to governments to spy on those such as terrorists working against governments. *The*

*Washington Post*, *The Guardian* and *The Wire* have published stories that Pegasus has been allegedly engaged by many countries to snoop on thousands of people around the world, including prominent state leaders.

Hundreds of prominent Indians – dissidents, journalists, central ministers, present and former government functionaries, including former CBI director Alok Verma and ex-election commissioner Ashok Lavasa, among others – are believed to be on the list. And more names are being revealed every day. What is puzzling is that some are the allies of the ruling party and others are its strident critics.

## Who hired NSO?

The question that haunts many Indians since the government has denied any role in hiring the services of NSO is: who paid it to do the dirty job?

NSO is not a charitable 'not-for-profit' company or NGO. It begs further questions if the government has washed its hands off. Could it be that the intelligence agencies, which have immense resources, have overstepped their authority and hired Pegasus keeping the government in the dark, as was the case when senior officials of the National Security Council went beyond their brief in the Iran-Contra scandal that rocked US President Ronald Reagan's second presidency and like the Inter-Services Intelligence (ISI) in Pakistan, which often acts as an independent deep state?

It cannot also be ruled out that if the government is unaware of the activities of NSO, countries inimical to India like China or Pakistan could have engaged Pegasus through proxy companies to spy on top Indian government leaders.

It is well known that Russia was suspected of using its highly sophisticated and powerful intelligence agencies to spy on Donald Trump and the Democrats during the run-up to the US elections in 2016. China, like Russia and the United States, has also independent capabilities to use its spyware to snoop on Indian political leaders, including those in power.

The government may claim it is not spying on others, but it could itself be the target of the spyware by unknown countries. If even President Emmanuel Macron of France is the target of Pegasus spyware, the top brass of the Indian government should be worried.

In such a scenario, if the government is absolved of this alleged shameful act of hiring a foreign agency to spy on its cabinet colleagues and allies and other citizens who are critical of it, it is all the more urgent and important to order an independent probe to get to the bottom of this sordid and dangerous affair and determine which foreign country is snooping on us.

Earlier, the Congress government also brazenly abused its powers to allegedly spy on its cabinet ministers, political opponents and citizens indiscriminately. During UPA II, it was reported that every month 7,000–8,000 new phone numbers of suspected citizens were added to the list of numbers to be brought under surveillance by the home ministry.

State governments were and are no exception. As Seshadri Chari, an RSS acolyte and former editor of *Organiser*, wrote surprisingly in *The Print*, the government must be held to account so that an independent non-partisan inquiry is held to determine who hired Pegasus. It is paramount for national integrity and security.

There is a well-known Buddhist proverb, 'To every man is given the key to the gates of heaven; the same key opens the gates of hell.' The spyware is like the key. The leader of a country can use the same spyware for good to snoop on enemies of the state or use it abominably on their unsuspecting citizens – political opponents, critics as well as colleagues in the government to keep them in check and fear through surveillance.

Spying on someone can also be a queer fetish like that of 'Peeping Tom'. When you feel you have unbridled power to snoop on anyone and everyone, the deep roots of it are likely salacious in origin. As Henry Kissinger famously quipped, 'Power is the ultimate aphrodisiac.'

*Moneycontrol*, July 2021

# The Yogi and the Prince

The first is a 'yogi' in the making. The recurring images of 2021 are those of Prime Minister Narendra Modi in a striking, cascading snowy beard framed by a luxuriant white mane, launching events and election rallies – still a veritable lion in spring. An image makeover from a tough, muscular administrator, an astute politician, the unquestioned party supremo and a much-adored and feared ruler, to an elder sage, not entirely a saint, but a Raj Rishi – still reigning over matters of state, with the reins firmly in his hand – is a big political gamble.

His fans on social media share his pictures with words of raving adulation, juxtaposing him alongside the towering figure of the poet laureate of Bengal, Rabindranath Tagore; in Tamil Nadu, he must seem like Periyar, and in Pondicherry, like the mystic Shri Aurobindo. It is like looking at some ancient paintings and temple sculptures where the same figure takes on different forms when viewed from different angles by the beholder. If Modi had the current round of elections in mind when he decided to embark on this transformation, it is sheer marketing genius, requiring foresight, insight and advanced planning to go from his clipped white beard and well-groomed visage, which had already propelled him to the heights of a demigod, to this sagely figure.

It is also fraught with political risks. Who can divine the mind of the public? It is inscrutably fickle. Will those who loved a strong, muscular leader – on which premise Modi's image was assiduously built over decades – accept a new, softer, sapient being, a persona now portrayed in complete contrast to the former?

The problem with strong leaders is that over time, they develop opaque vision and don't see what everyone else can see. They become cocksure. As Bertrand Russell said, 'Nobody should be certain of anything. If you're certain, you're certainly wrong, because nothing deserves certainty.' A lack of certainty, being unsure and accepting dilemmas, is necessary in a leader as it will make them humble and impel them to seek wider consultations and reduce committing grave errors. But history bears out that strong leaders cast a spell on their people. Will Modi, going forward, consult widely, in keeping with the new image he is morphing into?

From time immemorial, Indians have had a special fascination for sadhus, babas, swamis, maharishis, gurus and the like. That world is full of charlatans and crooks. It has also been blessed with many noble souls. Modi's moment of epiphany – to fashion himself into a sanyasi – may have come when he went to the cave in Kedarnath. If you visit the Himalayas and sit on a peak and watch the sun rise or behold the Ganga in the higher reaches at sunset, you too will wish to just walk away forever from this base material world and dissolve in the mountain mist.

So, this dramatic transformation from a commissar who justified all means to achieve ends for his country to a yogi who has transcended all mundane and corporeal grossness of life, who is in the thick of venal politics and yet floating above it like the lotus flower, the symbol of the BJP, is an apt metaphor. The imagery is perfect. Will the people embrace Modi in the new avatar? Only time will tell.

At the other end of the spectrum, you have Rahul Gandhi, the prince who is not able to shake off the image of a dilettante, of an easy-going dynast with privileges and entitlement – an image that has stuck to him. He comes across as more of a perennial Prince Hamlet, forever dilly-dallying and postponing. Nehru was suave, a great thinker, but he was not a ditherer, never suffered fools and did not let emotions and sentiment make him squeamish. Many feel that Rahul doesn't seem to inspire his cadre and seems to lack that killer instinct his opponents possess to lead a political party. Napoleon once said, 'I'm no capuchin' (I'm no saint). An Italian proverb says, 'If you wish to succeed, you must not be too good.' Emerson, speaking of Napoleon, said, 'Napoleon renounced, once for all, sentiments and affections, and would help himself with his hand and his head … it's an advantage, within certain limits, to have renounced the dominion of sentiments, of gratitude and generosity; since what was an impassable bar to us, and others, becomes a convenient weapon for our purposes …'

Rahul Gandhi's recent interviews and interactions with economists, intellectuals and reputed foreign universities reveal him as a decent, relatively young man with knowledge and maturity. He is no 'Pappu', nor an imbecile, as made out by his opponents. He has wit and a sense of repartee. He is a bugbear and a gadfly who continues to bite Modi, and Modi can't shake him off. He attracts crowds and media attention as he and his family name still have charisma with large sections of the population. He is seen as the only fierce and consistent critic of Modi from the Opposition. The rest are conspicuous by their silence.

He seems strong as a Sherpa, accomplished in martial arts, and he has displayed phenomenal fitness on stage, competing with young athletes and besting them easily. Yet, for all his discreet attempts at image transformation, he is perceived as weak, while Modi is seen as strong. Rahul's ambivalence when it comes to leading his party and his equivocation on many issues seem stark in contrast to the shrewd mercilessness, swiftness and purposive actions of not just Modi but of his own grandmother, Indira Gandhi.

Will the image change that Rahul is attempting crystallize in the minds of the populace? Will it count with the voters? Can the people decipher the precise man that he is? Will he be able to steer the Congress out of its morass and unseat Modi as the latter changes his own persona and reinvents himself? We have to wait and see.

It's not enough to 'Know thyself'. To win a battle, you must 'Know thy enemy,' as Sun Tzu said. Maybe, Rahul must study Modi.

*Deccan Herald*, March 2021

# All the Waters of the Ganga

Uttar Pradesh, the hallowed land of sacred rivers and holy temples and of sadhus and saints, has become a map of rape and death. All the waters of the Ganga will not wash the blood and cleanse the sins of the perpetrators of the rape of the Dalit girl in Hathras, nor all its holy waters purify the defenders of rapists and their lusty cheerleaders. The rapists and killers may hang or may go scot-free under political patronage, but can those in ochre robes who wield power, where criminals under their watch have a free run, those leaders who sing *Vande Mataram* and end their speeches with zesty cries of *Bharatmata ki Jai*, can they go unpunished? Can any amount of worship in the temples of Kashi and singing and chanting of beads in Mathura to appease the gods exculpate them from their dastardly crimes when they violate women with such cruelty? Can such a land ever aspire to Ram Rajya?

Why did the UP government busy itself in pointing fingers at Rahul and Priyanka Gandhi or assaulting and arresting journalists and civil rights activists who were showing solidarity with the victim's family? If there is such a rape or murder in West Bengal, shouldn't the BJP protest against the administration of Mamata Banerjee? If there are violent sexual assaults and brutalization of

Dalits in Rajasthan, as has been the case, can the BJP sit quiet and let Ashok Gehlot off the hook?

Doesn't the UP government realize that its soft-pedalling of atrocities against Dalit women and high-handedness and exploitation of minorities will be taken as tacit approval of these by the upper castes and will result in a backlash against them and against the BJP itself and its affiliates, as has happened in West Bengal and Kerala previously, where they are at the receiving end? The autocratic ways of Mayawati when she rode roughshod, channelling Dalit anger against upper castes gave way to lumpen elements from the Yadav community and Muslim leaders during the rule of Mulayam and Akhilesh Yadav. Did not the BJP ride to power promising to rid Uttar Pradesh of violence and goondaism, on the promise of good governance?

Some political commentators have observed that 'While Muslims as "enemies" suits the BJP's political strategy perfectly, alienating the Dalit vote could exact a heavy price.' Uma Bharti has been openly critical of the Yogi government's handling of the Hathras rape and assault. Others have commented that while Muslim lives might not matter for the BJP, Dalits' lives matter. Their votes do. They have warned that Yogi is playing with fire, stoking it to appease the upper castes. Is this the time to descend to such depths, to dissect caste calculations and vote bank arithmetic? We cannot be more depraved than this. Every life matters. Every daughter is inviolate. Be it a Dalit or a Muslim, a Thakur or a Jat, a Brahmin or a Baniya.

When Nirbhaya was raped and murdered bestially during UPA rule, no one asked what caste she belonged to. The whole country rose in one voice against the brutal sexual assault on her. The BJP rightly joined the protests of the students and youth and held the UPA government to account and demanded that our cities be made safe. Maybe the BJP exploited the situation by dipping into the anger of the people and derived political mileage from the Nirbhaya episode and hastened the demise of the UPA regime. The Congress, which is being accused of 'politicizing' the Hathras rape and murder, may be doing the same. Now, the boot is on the other foot. The Yogi government must be held responsible for the lawlessness in Uttar

Pradesh. The writing is on the wall. Uttar Pradesh is not safe for women. Any woman.

The latest National Crime Records Bureau figures show that in India, 88 women are raped every day, out of which 10 are Dalit women. Uttar Pradesh holds the dubious record, laying claim to 14.7 per cent of all crimes against women in the country. Yogi was handpicked to emancipate the state, free it of violence against women and unshackle its people from the grip of the Samajwadi Party and its hoodlums. Sadly, the state has simply passed from the hands of the goons of one party into the arms of the thugs of the next. This has been the fate of the people of the state over the last few decades, with no respite from atrocities, social instability, conflict and strife.

Can this be the land of Tulsidas' *Ramcharitmanas*, considered widely the highest essence of our culture, that eulogises the noblest ideals and deeds of Rama, the very epitome of glorious Indian devotional poetry of universal love, where now terror reigns and rapists stalk the land and where women fear to tread outside their homes? Our mythology places women over men, gives them precedence as we worship and chant their names, Radha-Krishna, Siya–Ram, ParvatiParameshwara, who are invoked as the embodiment of Shakti, Durga and Kali who ward off evil so that in flesh and blood, we may hold our daughters, sisters and mothers in awe and reverence. Tulsidas wrote the epic poem in vernacular Awadh Hindi, shorn of high-flown poetic Sanskrit, synthesising it from many versions of the Ramayana and stories from the Puranas so that the ethos of Sita and Rama could reach and suffuse the common people and ennoble them in their daily deeds and prayers.

It should be a people's good fortune when a 'Yogi' becomes the 'King' of his state. For he is supposed to combine in himself the virtues of an ascetic and attributes of a just ruler who administers through dharma, what Atal Behari Vajpayee eloquently called Raj Dharma. It would be a great misfortune if it were to be otherwise in Uttar Pradesh, as has been the case so far.

*Deccan Herald*, October 2020

# Why Prashant Bhushan's Trial for Contempt Should Be Declared a Mistrial

I'm not a jurist. But some things are self-evident. A fundamental premise in law is 'you cannot try yourself', let alone try those with whom you're conflicted.

Let me narrate a story from my army days. While I was posted in a training establishment in a Defence Recruitment and Training Centre, which took in soldiers who retired at an early age from the army for rehabilitation to be trained and posted again in non-combatant roles as security guards in defence installations, I came across a recruit with a strange case history. Before joining my establishment, he was summarily court-martialled, discharged from the army and sent to prison to serve a sentence of six months by the commanding officer of the battalion where he served. He was charged with sexually molesting the daughter of the commanding officer, with the rank of a lieutenant colonel, who had summary court-martial powers. The soldier went to the high court and challenged the sentencing. The court set aside the judgment as the rules clearly stipulated that a commanding officer cannot try cases in which he's involved and is conflicted. The soldier was released from prison and he rejoined the army.

Now, I'm not talking about the bizarre case of a former Chief Justice who presided over a hearing arising from sexual harassment charges against himself – one of the instances of 'corruption' in the widest sense of the word that Prashant Bhushan speaks about in his reply to the Supreme Court, running into hundreds of pages which the court ignored – but a larger problem.

While the charges Bhushan made through his tweets (and interview in 2009) are directed at individual judges whose conduct, in his opinion, undermines the judiciary and shakes the pillars of democracy; one does not need to be a legal luminary to make out that the conflict is between Bhushan and the Supreme Court.

Here, I'm not arguing over the merits of the court's order convicting Bhushan for his tweets but about the legal and moral sanctity of the trial itself. In putting Bhushan on trial for criminal contempt on the charge of scandalizing the court, the Supreme Court is, in effect, standing in judgment of itself.

The charge of 'scandalizing the court' should have been scrapped long ago, or at least when the Law Commission suggested its deletion recently. The 'crime' Bhushan has been convicted of is archaic, anachronistic and monarchic in its origins. Whosoever is delusional enough to think he or she is a law unto themselves – be it an elected leader, a bureaucrat, a police officer, or a judge – will, by definition, be intolerant of those who dissent and disagree and who walk their own path. Anyone who thinks like an emperor has no place in a democracy. As Emerson said, 'Difference of opinion is one crime emperors never forgive.'

Even if we accept the bench's reasoning that it acted *suo motu* against Bhushan and that the original complainant's failure to obtain the attorney general's consent – as mandated by the Contempt of Courts Act, 1971 – was not a flaw; my view is that what we saw was not a fair and just trial but a mistrial. A court that insists on judging the subjective charge that someone has 'scandalized it' lacks credibility and is suspect, irrespective of the credentials of the judges.

The Supreme Court is 'supreme' and can adjudicate on all matters between various third parties. Incontrovertible. But can it be an arbiter in cases where it is, de facto, an accused, as in the instant case? Surely it cannot.

We must all remember there are now five pillars of democracy, not four. Elected representatives, the executive, the judiciary, the press or the fourth estate and now the public at large, turbo-charged with the power of the Internet, where millions can directly express their thoughts and which potentially has a far wider reach and potency than newspapers and television. The court of public opinion – the fifth pillar of democracy, supreme in its own way – cannot and must not be overlooked but should guide the other four pillars in taking informed decisions while delivering on their oath of office.

Humility serves all, especially when we are likely to be blinded by sanctimonious virtue, ego and power. Judges are human like us. The Supreme Court must gracefully find a way out of the impasse it finds itself presently in, enlisting the help of the AG and the bar.

Eventually, it must frame new laws and rules to set right the conundrum that the Prashant Bhushan Contempt Case has posed to prevent abuse of the fundamental tenet: No one can be a judge in her/his own case or cause. This is true of a single judge, and the court is happy to concede this. But the charge of 'scandalizing the court' thrusts the court itself into the role of judge in its own case. And this is surely incompatible with natural justice.

Beyond the ego and fate of individuals, the Bhushan case has raised paramount questions of democracy. At stake are liberty and justice. And as Edmund Burke said, 'Whenever a separation is made between liberty and justice, neither, in my opinion, is safe.'

*The Wire*, August 2020

# In the Land of Myriad Gods, Whose Temples Will We Choose to Build?

As I watched the grand foundation-laying ceremony of the Rama temple in Ayodhya on 5 August 2020, my mind wandered back in time to my village Gorur, where I grew up. Images of temples, gods on palanquins, priests and temple music flickered past my mind's eye.

As you entered the picturesque village, you first saw a magnificent old peepul tree (also called Bodhi tree), around which many idols of snakes were placed. The women of the village perambulated around the sacred tree, lit oil lamps and incense sticks and applied vermilion to the totems of snakes and other figurines that are symbols of fertility.

There were a couple of neem trees adjacent to the peepul trees on the same platform, a common sight in all villages in the old Mysore province. Parents of unmarried women planted and nurtured the twin trees and carried out a marriage ceremony between them, a hoary ritual that gave hope that the woman in the family would soon be betrothed. And as you walked past the peepul tree, at the entrance to the village, you came upon a tiny temple with twin deities – a Hanuman facing west and a Maramma looking south (the predominant female goddess in the rural southern parts of Karnataka and Tamil Nadu believed to protest against disease and pestilence and be the harbinger of rains).

The village had three other main temples. There was Yoga Narasimha at the edge of the village to the south on the bank of the Hemavati river, a Shiva temple on the northern periphery and another Paravasudeva temple to the west abutting the Agrahara, the Brahmin quarters. And there was one more very powerful deity that resided about two kilometres downstream called Banadamma – a forest goddess, a wood spirit, as the name suggests – residing in a grove.

Along with Shiva and Vishnu avatar temples, every village had many female deities and a Puradamma – a female goddess. All these temples and small abodes of worship were from antiquity. In Gorur, we did not have a Rama temple. No elders could explain why some villages had a Rama temple, and the others had Narasimha, Narayana, Krishna or Keshava deities; they brushed it aside, saying they were all the manifestations of one god, Vishnu.

While all villages had Shiva temples and Vishnu temples that were administered by upper castes, and the devotees of one did not frequent the other, the lives of tribals, Dalits and other backward class (OBC) members largely revolved around their family goddesses of Maramma, Banadamma and Puradamma. Rama, Krishna or Vishnu did not dominate their lives.

While people of the village and surrounding hamlets freely and frequently visited the Gorur Narasimha Swamy temple, the deity which was also the presiding deity for the annual wooden car festival that attracted tens of thousands of devotees of all castes and communities, during ordinary days throughout the year, the Dalits and backward castes, who constituted a larger number of the populace, worshipped the lesser-known female deities, made vows and offered animal sacrifices and feasted after the puja rituals. Rama, Krishna and Vishnu, the main gods of the Hindu pantheon, were not their deities in times of distress or calamity, or while taking vows for fulfilling their secret prayers.

The choice of a temple or a particular 'god', who is believed to be more powerful and propitiating than the other gods with legends and lores, is oxymoronic. The Tirupati Balaji temple, a Vishnu temple managed by a government trust, the Dharmasthala Temple of Manjunatha, a private Shiva temple under the trusteeship of Jains, the hallowed temples of Kollur Mookambika and the Shirdi Saibaba temple, worshipped by mainly Hindus but also Muslims, the Aiyappa temple in Shabarmalai, the Siddhivinayaka temple in Mumbai, the Kashi Vishwanath temple and many more are largely a recent phenomenon of the middle class, the Hindu bourgeois and the nouveau riche, film stars and politicians seeking security and rewards. Superstitions that are given currency between competing deities are commercializing, belittling and trivializing the gods, but are grist to the mill of the trusts that manage the temples. But the marginalized and the poor have a benign indifference to these celebrity temple deities in distant towns. They go about their lives stoically and seek refuge, solace and strength in their local goddesses.

I recall when I contested an election for the state legislature in Hassan district, my co-workers insisted that I must begin my campaign by first visiting a famous female deity in my constituency, deep in the rural wilderness, and offer prayers along with them. They took me in a procession and asked me to make a wish as I prayed to the goddess sitting in the sanctum to bless me and give me a sign by the first flower dropping to her side, the side that I had chosen. I was asked to offer a lamb in sacrifice and host a feast.

Though sceptical, I readily acquiesced, eager to clutch at any straw that took me to the shores of victory. After the goddess gave the signal of my assured victory through the drop of a flower on the side I had opted, and after I had a good repast made out of the sacrificial lamb, we hit the campaign trail. And when the results showed that I had suffered a resounding defeat, trounced by my rival who had also visited the same shrine; I wondered why my party workers did not take me to a famous Rama, Krishna or a Shiva temple but led me to an obscure goddess in the woods. My faith was shaken, but not theirs.

While poor Dalits, backward castes and tribals rarely visited the temples of Rama or Krishna, they nevertheless zestfully performed mythological dramas from the Mahabharata and Ramayana in open-air theatres after the harvesting season, going on all night. They trained under an itinerant drama master, well-versed in the epics and mythological Puranas, who taught them by rote. There was no script. It was an oral and aural tradition passed down across generations. And therefore the practise went on for three to four months.

The actors, the poorest of the poor, who took part (and often vied with one another for heroic parts) had to pay to cover the cost of the drama teacher and the costumes, stage, lighting and sound system. The practice sessions started after the day's labours, in the central courtyard of the village, and lasted late into the night. The folk songs from the epics accompanied by the hum of a harmonium would waft across the fields to my cottage not far away and brought tears to my eyes, and my heart swelled. It was not a religious act. It was a sublime act of love and worship to perpetuate a folk art the community instinctively clung on to.

As these images and thoughts from bygone times crowded my mind, I reflected, what will the new Rama temple, when completed three years from now, signify to those millions who toil daily on farms and fields and on shop floors, factories and construction sites? The middle class and the rich will add Ayodhya to the pilgrim circuit and travel by cars, planes and trains – as they do now to Kashi, Haridwar, Badrinath, Kedarnath – and offer prayers to seek prosperity and success in their undertakings, gorge on savouries and sweets and pollute the earth, water and sky like the other pilgrim towns that are choking the rivers and streams with filth and garbage.

Many of these temple circuits of the modern Indian are more about revelry than pilgrimage of piety. The rest of the two-thirds of the population, the amorphous Hindu with no allegiance to any particular god – the farmers, weavers, potters, fishermen, cowherds, shepherds, potters, stone cutters and earth diggers in their villages and the countless nameless labourers who were the invisible hands from across this vast land of myriad gods who provided for us and kept us warm, who have trudged back to their homes and may never return – will continue to sing and dance around their lesser-known, local gods and goddesses, and likely find deliverance through their work and worship.

As the high priests chanted Vedic hymns in praise of Lord Rama and bricks of stones and silver were laid, and pictures of hundreds of stone columns and pediments were flashed on television, a line from Rabindranath Tagore rang in my mind:

> 'When God waits for His temple to be built of love, men bring stones.'

*The Wire*, August 2020

# Chinese Capers in Ladakh – How to Stand Up to a Bully

My first border posting after the Bangladesh Liberation War in December 1971 was on the Chinese front in January 1972. At point 4752. There was no name to this peak that stood towering at 4,752 metres (15,586 feet above MSL) at Chola in the state of Sikkim, just a few kilometres along the border to the north of Nathu La. It was an observation post, the highest in the region, desolate and forbidding. It would be snowbound most of the year, with the maximum temperatures in summers being minus 2 to 3 degree centigrade and in winters dropping to minus 30 degrees centigrade. My concrete bunker was perched right atop 4752. A few metres below was the infantry battalion the Jammu and Kashmir Rifles (1st JaK Rif). I had my course mate second lieutenant G.D. Bakshi (now a retired major general, military historian, analyst and a well-known television face), irrepressible even then, posted there, who provided cheery company. When weather permitted, we would go down to the battalion mess to toast over an evening of rum. The Chinese were just 200 yards across the imaginary border that ran across a lake that remained frozen in winter. 4752 was a four-hour trek from Changu Lake at 10,000 feet, where my regiment was headquartered. I stayed on that outpost for fifteen months.

But first, a few words about the Bangladesh Liberation War which are relevant to this story on the skirmishes between China and India in Ladakh Galwan River valley and Pangong Tso lake along the line of actual control (LAC) and the continuing standoff, which has now escalated and resulted in the fatalities of two Indian soldiers along with one commanding officer and five Chinese soldiers, though these are not yet officially confirmed.

My batch in the Indian Military Academy (IMA) acquired the sobriquet 'Born To Battle' because in September 1971, while still undergoing training, the course was abruptly cut short, and 150 of us officers, all of twenty years of age, were dispatched post-haste to the front to join our respective regiments and battalions. There were reports of mobilization and build-up of troops and tanks and artillery along the borders both on the Western and Eastern Front as a sea of refugees from East Pakistan (now Bangladesh) poured into the border states of India. And war was in the air. On the train to Siliguri, where I was headed to join my unit, the 52 Mountain Regiment, located on the borders with China in Sikkim's high-altitude region, a palpable, strange sensation and excitement ran through the crowd of soldiers as they discussed animatedly the titbits of information they had gathered from their units on the front. I arrived at Siliguri station early evening in late September and boarded a long convoy of army jeeps and trucks that wound their way up through the majestic Himalayan mountains as dusk enveloped us. After ten days of acclimatization in transit camps along the way via Gangtok, I reached my battery headquarters in the Changu Lake area at eight on a freezing night. The still lake, surrounded by lofty, snow-capped mountains piercing the sky, glistened under a moonlit sky. The mystic, awe-inspiring Kanchenjunga soared above them all to the north.

It was an enchanting sight, but beneath there were rumblings of war. As I was ushered into the regimental camp and was greeted by a young senior subaltern to show me to my bunkered quarters, there was a hubbub of people milling around. The unit was astir, packing and loading trucks. The lieutenant told me that the regiment, along with the mountain division, had received mobilization orders the previous day and the entire unit would leave early morning the next day along with all the guns, ammunition and complements to the plains for the Bangla front under the 33 Corps headquartered in Siliguri. I was speechless with the suddenness of the events. I was expecting to move to my picket on 4752 but was now heading back in the next few hours.

I didn't sleep a wink the whole night. The constant shuffling of the boots of the soldiers, the hum of low voices, the sound of the howling wind and my own thoughts of the events that were unfolding kept me awake. My unpacked bags were loaded again and at the crack of dawn, we rolled down the mountains in a long convoy of vehicles, back toward Siliguri, which is located on the narrow passage resembling a chicken neck between Bhutan and Bangladesh, connecting West Bengal to the north-eastern states of India.

Before I was able to collect my thoughts and settle down, we plunged headlong into East Pakistan as the Indian Army invaded from multiple fronts. We were engulfed in war on both fronts – East and West Pakistan. Events overtook us so swiftly, with close to ten million refugees crossing the borders into India, that not going into war was not an option for India. It was a blitzkrieg invasion, and I moved along a battery of guns with my regiment as we moved in step with the Infantry Brigade deep into Dinajpur in the then East Pakistan. The war was won in fifteen days, and the Pakistan Army was crushed, with a hundred thousand soldiers taken prisoner. Bangladesh, a new nation, came into being. It was the courageous and decisive leadership of Mrs Indira Gandhi with a clear mandate to the Indian Army, and the charismatic military genius of Field Marshal Manekshaw, who led a great intrepid army that had built itself into a well-trained, well-knit and better-equipped professional force after the lessons from the Chinese war of 1962, that delivered a resounding victory to India against Pakistan.

The Bangladesh victory and the leadership both at the political and military level have valid and important lessons in the present context of the escalating standoff with China on the Ladakh border.

Without delving deep into the strategic and tactical analysis of the terrain and comparative analysis of our military prowess and infrastructure and logistics capabilities vis-à-vis China, in Ladakh and along our 4000-kilometre border with China (there are many accomplished military commanders and military historians who have written and are continuing to write about this), I wish to speak about some home truths. Battles have always been won since the time of Genghis Khan, Hannibal and Napoleon, who conquered vast territories stretching thousands of kilometres, whose smaller armies trounced bigger ones, only through superior planning, tactics, speed and elements of surprise, outflanking and outmanoeuvring. Napoleon said, 'It is not cannons but lightning that wins wars.' In his famous standoff with Mrs Gandhi, Sam Manekshaw, after he refused her orders to attack East Pakistan in June 1971 when she pressed him but he wished to wait until the December of that year, had said he had to keep China in his mind in his plans of invasion because in June, the snows would have melted in the valleys, making it passable and easier for China to march into Indian territory, and this could open a third front. He preferred December for the attack for many tactical and strategic reasons and also because it gave them time for mobilizing. The harsh winter with the snow-bound valleys on the heights would deter the Chinese from embarking on any misadventure. The lightning speed, combined with elements of surprise and decisive political and military leadership, won India the Bangladesh Liberation War despite fighting on two fronts with Pakistan and the threat of exposure to a third from China.

There were two other earlier occasions when prompt and decisive retaliation by the Indian Army commanders had forced the Chinese to beat a hasty withdrawal after provocative incursions into Indian territory. At the very height of the India–Pakistan war of 1965, in September, Chairman Mao issued an ultimatum to withdraw from Nathu La on the Sikkim border with Tibet, but Major General Sagat Singh, the divisional commander, stood firm and defiant and made it known by putting his troops on high alert to repulse any Chinese mischief. And again, in August 1967, China renewed its claims on Nathu La and attempted to cross over the LAC, accompanied by machine-gun fire to browbeat the Indian Army. General Sagat Singh, who was still the divisional commander, losing no time, mobilized the artillery, mortars and machine guns and pounded the encroaching Chinese, inflicting heavy casualties. India, too, lost troops but suffered fewer fatalities. And once again, in the summer of 1986, when Chinese troops made incursions in Tawang, laying claims to the Wangdung grazing ground in Arunachal (the area interestingly close to the Namitha Chu Valley where, in 1962, the Chinese People's Liberation Army (PLA) had overwhelmed the unprepared Indian troops), Major General Jimmy Singh, the divisional commander, moved his troops in a flash and mobilized mortars and gave discretion to the local commanders to use the fire power at their disposal to stop any Chinese intrusions. Lieutenant General Narahari, the IV Corps commander in Arunachal (who was my brigade commander during my army days and also later, after retirement, the chairman of Air Deccan), sprang into action and gave orders to deploy infantry battalions swiftly. And General Sundarji, the then army chief, when General Jimmy requested 1,200 mules to build up supplies and fortifications with mountain guns to defend Tawang, said it was no time for mules and gave heavy-lift Russian helicopters for airlifting artillery guns. The Chinese, realizing the massive build-up and likely heavy retaliation, withdrew.

These episodes are well documented by many (notably by military analysts Maroof Raja and Air Vice Marshal Arjun Subramaniam recently), and when many years ago I asked Lieutenant General Narahari about his storied commandeering of artillery and large-scale troops to stave off a Chinese attack reminiscent of 1962, he confirmed the incidents and said, 'You have to act boldly with firmness and take proactive and pre-emptive action to stop infiltration. You are not posted there to be caught with your pants down and then report to Delhi and seek permission to drive out the invaders.' When General Sundarji was asked by the then Prime Minister if it was not hasty to mobilize the army; the flamboyant Sundarji is reported to have quipped, 'I've just done my job, Sir. Now it's up to you to do yours.'

The moot point is that in the Operations Manuals and Guidelines for military commanders on the field, all levels of command are very clearly defined and laid out, and they are expected to use their discretion in repulsing enemy incursions by choosing appropriate and timely tactical responses. They are also required to keep their higher command in the loop. The borders are manned and patrolled to prevent incursions, with enough leeway for the local commanders to use force as deemed appropriate. The problem arises when there is ambiguity in enunciating a clear strategy at the political level and when there's prevarication and pussyfooting by the political leadership, taking away the discretion of army commanders on the field to act decisively when the enemy encroaches on your territory. When the field commanders then begin looking over their shoulders to get approvals and by the time it travels up the chain to the bureaucrats in the Ministry of Defence, who will, in turn, analyse matters to death and then get political sanction from the defence minister, who is hamstrung and diffident because he, in turn, has to confer with the Prime Minister and the national security agency (NSA), and by the time they wake up it is too late as the chickens will have come home to roost by then. And the enemy will have entrenched himself, making eviction more complex and difficult. This is not to suggest recklessness and trigger a war. The army commanders cannot *suo moto* invade a neighbouring country, but they are not expected to seek permission from the higher authorities to repel enemy incursion into Indian territory. That will be abdicating their core responsibility.

Many highly decorated retired army generals and defence analysts of repute have pointed out that successive governments have been tardy and have failed in building matching or adequate armament capabilities of the three forces in step with China, which has taken a leap, and our arms procurement from tendering to field trials and financial closure still takes ten to fifteen years and is disgraceful and purchases are rushed through knee-jerk bilaterals under direct government-to-government contracts as has now become the norm, which is not a desirable way of acquisition, and the Make In India for defence armaments is still a shoddy affair and remains a chimera. Despite this, the Indian Army, Navy and Air Force have over the years acquired immense capabilities in a conventional war with China and, in mountain warfare, it is the best in the world, and there's wide consensus that India has an edge over China if a full-scale war breaks out. And the terrain is to India's advantage. Let us bear in mind that the entire border with China is with Tibet, an annexed territory and in any warfare, China has to contend with a Tibetan population that is inimical to it and is seeking to free itself from China and will back India in a full-fledged war. Indian troops are the best trained and motivated in the world and have over 200 years of war experience from Mesopotamia, Afghan wars and World War I and II, among others, and have won laurels and high praise. All these should put China on the back foot regardless of its posturing. But I wish to emphasize that even if we did not have these advantages, the way to deal with a bully is not the way India has chosen.

It is an ancient truism that bullies are cowards and lack in self-esteem, be it nations or individuals. Every schoolboy knows that if you let a bully browbeat you, he's going to do it again. There is only one proven and effective way to take on a bully. You must stand up to him. Your rage against his bullying ways and your determination to stand up and fight him to the end will ensure his hasty retreat. 'When you brave death, you drive him into the enemy's camp,' said Napoleon. Armies that resolve to win always win. The old adage that 'It's not the size of the dog in the fight, it's the size of the fight in the dog that matters' still holds true.

When China realizes that the moment they dance along our borders, intruding in and out at will, its capers will turn out to be a dance of death and each such incursion will be met with instant, heavy retaliation and that they cannot hope to annexe even an inch of land from India from across the LAC unless they fight a full-fledged war with, and risk a Tibetan uprising, they will stop playing these bullying games.

*The Times of India*, June 2020

# Congress Must Move Away from Hero Worship and Towards Intra-Party Democracy

Most societies, born often out of superstition or out of historical, religious and cultural processes, cling on to symbols and totems that are of special spiritual or personal significance, much like the 'fertility totems' of indigenous people. All of them have some origins and associations with natural phenomena, hoary rituals or ancestry.

For the Congress, it's ancestry. The Nehru–Gandhi family is its totem. Over the years, successive coteries of courtiers and sycophants have cast a voodoo spell on Congress workers down the line, with those closest to the Gandhis dancing around the 'Gandhi totem pole'.

The majority of these minions and hangers-on derived their power through the family, and the Gandhi talisman was necessary for their own survival and for keeping the party together. They stood to gain by perpetuating the myth. Implicit in this act of worship was the message that discarding their lucky charm would spell doom for the party. And the ruling family readily embraced the idea.

Now Rahul Gandhi has resigned. And the devotees are utterly bereft, like the faithful who feel orphaned when their godman or cult leader is whisked away from the ashram and put away in jail for crimes that they believed only ordinary mortals like themselves could commit.

Rahul Gandhi did the right and courageous thing by standing firm and not yielding to emotional pressures to return to the kind of cult that the Congress dynastic rule had morphed into. He has set an example by accepting electoral defeat and holding himself accountable and has walked away. And he has walked away tall.

Therein lies the central message for India's grand old party – there is, or should be, no place for hero worship. No one, not even the 'superhero', is exempt from being held to account. A few years ago, Rahul Gandhi had tried to galvanize the party bottom-up from the grassroots, trying to usher in a new era of politics through organizational elections across the country, but it excluded himself. That rule also did not apply to his mother, Sonia Gandhi, or members of the top coterie that had surrounded them, the ones who had come to acquire extra-constitutional authority in the party and government during the Congress's rule over the years.

The elections acted as a clarion call. The sentiment was increasingly reflective of the fact that, yes, all were equal, but some were more equal than others. This now bordered on the comic and sounded hollow, and Rahul's attempts to enforce a sense of equality fizzled out.

Yes, he should have quit earlier, but it is never too late. It is not easy to simply walk away from the throne. The fawning disciples make it impossible. It has to be admired that he has done it now, and he is resolute. Rahul's detailed letter is a good starting point.

Now the deadwood needs cleaning up through genuine organizational elections. Fresh blood and ideas need to be breathed in by attracting people who genuinely believe in the ideals of Mahatma Gandhi, Nehru, Sardar Patel and other stalwarts. It will be a long haul and an arduous task, but it is the only way to save the Congress, which is necessary for a robust democracy when there's hardly any opposition to count on. Just as a vibrant opposition to the Congress was the need after Independence.

The Congress does not have to go far to take lessons – they just need to look at the party's own illustrious history of over 134 years. Many eminent people who were titans of their time, including foreigners, have been presidents of the party. Gokhale, Mahatma Gandhi, Sarojini Naidu, Chittaranjan Das, Maulana Azad, Madam Mohan Malaviya, Lala Lajpat Rai, Annie Besant, Subhas Chandra Bose, Motilal Nehru, Jawaharlal Nehru and Sardar Patel are just a few names of those who led the party.

From its very inception, the party believed in genuine democracy, diversity and plurality of ideas and religions. That explains why it attracted so many luminaries and had such a huge following among the masses. Subhas Chandra Bose contested and won the presidential elections in 1938 and in 1939 when Mahatma Gandhi openly lobbied and worked hard to defeat Bose. Then, Purushottam Tandon, in 1949, backed by Sardar Patel, won the election to become the president even as Nehru opposed his nomination. This was the time when Nehru was the Prime Minister and Patel the home minister.

Gopal Gandhi, Mahatma Gandhi's grandson, had this to say in his op-ed in *The Hindu*:

> 'In that election (of Bose) and its aftermath lies another lesson for today's Congress. The party's new President should be elected as 'grandly' as Netaji was but she or he should not be treated as Netaji was, by the Gandhi-loyal Working Committee of the day. The new President should be left completely free to form the Working Committee, from out of persons whose service-mindedness not boss-mindfulness, is manifest … No leader will be found if the attempt is to find a dummy, not a leader. A dummy President will make a dummy of the party.'

Suhas Palshikar, political analyst and co-director of the Lokniti programme of the Centre for the Study of Developing Societies, has said that even though Jawaharlal Nehru was a towering figure in the Congress, his decisions involved and included compromises. 'Nehru allowed plurality of leaders. It was only after Indira came that dynasty took root in the Congress and the mantle was passed on to Rajiv,' Palshikar said.

Nehru, a historian himself, was not unaware of the dictatorial tendencies lurking inside him and the dangers of such a trait. He was the Congress president for nine terms and held that post even when he was the Prime Minister from 1950 to 1954 with vast powers vested in one man – himself.

Barring Maulana Azad, the tenures of most presidents were restricted to only one or two years. In 1937 when Nehru was elected Congress president for the fourth time, in a surprisingly candid article published in the same year in *Modern Review* and written under the pseudonym 'Chanakya' – unable, probably, to resist the temptations of power but yet troubled by it – he self-deprecatingly, said:

> 'From the far North to the Cape Comorin in the South he has gone like some triumphant Caesar passing by, leaving a trail of glory and a legend behind him. And yet he has all the makings of a dictator in him. … Caesarism is always at the door, and is it not possible that Jawaharlal might fancy himself a Caesar?'

It is the obligation of the committed Congress party workers who cherish and believe in its great values, traditions and sacrifices to introspect and set about in earnest to rebuild the party. The Gandhi family, who are ridiculed and accused of practising dynastic politics, cannot and ought not to be expected to set their house in order.

The crushing defeat in the recent parliamentary elections must be welcomed as a blessing in disguise by the Congress. They should take comfort in the fact that none of the other parties in the country has any semblance of genuine internal democracies, including the

BJP, and the Congress's history shows that the seeds of decline and degeneration were sown when the party adopted a dictatorial role.

No party in the country holds elections through a secret ballot for any post in the party at any level as was done in the Congress since it was founded and for a few years after Independence during Nehru's tenure.

The legislature party leaders who are chosen by the party to be appointed as chief ministers or the Prime Minister are never elected either, and not just by the Congress. The BJP claims it does not promote dynastic rule, but that does not mean it has internal party democracy.

Decisions are taken behind closed doors in party offices and five-star hotels and resorts, and multiple power centres, including the supposedly apolitical RSS, flex their muscles to appoint the president or leader of the party, who then are known to wield power till they are ousted in various inscrutable and non-transparent ways.

The regional parties are worse and are led by erratic megalomaniacs, who resemble many tinpot dictators of third world countries. A few of these regional parties are also brazenly dynastic.

We have a curious paradox. All parties, when in opposition, demand free and fair elections and swear by democracy, but strangely none of them care for intra-party democracy. Can we have true democracy in the country without genuine democracy within parties?

Democracy, in that respect, is modern and scientific. Yes, it is messed up, but an admission of ignorance – that no one has the perfect answer – is important because progress is possible only when there is freedom of thought.

When asked why scientists cannot solve societal problems, physicist and Nobel laureate Richard Feynman very eloquently said, 'If we take everything into account – not only what the ancients knew, but all of what we know today that they didn't know – then I think we must frankly admit that we do not know.' The leaders should sometimes admit that they do not know.

But increasingly, both at the state and Centre, no party in India encourages debate or tolerates dissent. Such a state of affairs does not bode well for the progress of either the state or any party in the long term.

In the prevailing political culture, the pervading absence of any ethics and total degeneration – which was also the cause of the downfall of the Congress – is, in fact, an opportune time for new leadership to emerge, from within the Congress, to slowly and steadfastly rebuild an organization on the ideals that great leaders like Gokhale, Gandhi, Bose, Nehru, Patel and others exemplified because it will be sure to rise again to shape the destiny of the country. It will not be without challenges or difficulties, but it will be a worthy effort.

*The Wire*, July 2019

# A Democracy We Can't Keep

When Benjamin Franklin, one of the Founding Fathers of the United States, was asked after a session of the Constitutional Convention, 'What kind of a government have you given us, republic or monarchy?' he is said to have replied, 'A republic, if you can keep it.'

If you survey the internal affairs of our major political parties, you begin to wonder if they are all personal fiefdoms of self-styled monarchs. Can we keep our republic, our democracy, if our political parties are little monarchies or dictatorships? It is common knowledge that since the Indira Gandhi era began, chief ministers have become puppets on a string, and the elected representatives of the people have been relegated to being mere pawns of their parties.

What is common to all our political parties? They all have a 'high command' that takes unilateral decisions. It may be a family dynasty like in the Congress, a 'supreme leader' surrounded by a coterie of one or two like in the Bharatiya Janata Party (BJP) or a single autocrat, as in the case of Mamata Banerjee of the All India Trinamool Congress (TMC) in Bengal, KC Chandrashekhar of Telangana Rashtra Samithi (TRS) in Telangana, M.K. Stalin of the Dravida Munnetra Kazhagam (DMK) in Tamil Nadu, Arvind

Kejriwal of Aam Aadmi Party (AAP) in Delhi or Deve Gowda of the Janata Dal (Secular) (JDS) in Karnataka. Like Louis XIV, they say, 'I am the party.' The party is their kingdom.

The supreme leaders of all parties are surrounded by a phalanx of courtiers and sycophants. Their job is to create echo chambers to reinforce and amplify their leader's voice. External ideas and diverse voices are shut out. This was best exemplified during United Progressive Alliance (UPA) II when the Congress high command lived in a bubble, cut off from reality while their palace gates were being breached and Narendra Modi was rising to power.

Let us begin with Congress, which is now drifting under a doddering dynasty incapable of steering the party through rough seas yet unwilling to let go of the wheel. Rahul Gandhi, who was anointed party president after much dithering, resigned in the wake of the Congress's dismal performance in the 2019 parliamentary elections. He abandoned his post without enabling an election to choose a successor or appointing to it someone from outside the family. The party is adrift under an ad hoc president, an ailing Sonia Gandhi, and now the troika of mother, son, and daughter Priyanka, without authority or accountability, is presiding over the destiny of a party fast disintegrating.

What do you make of Rahul Gandhi, who takes it upon himself to decide the fate of Sachin Pilot, the rebel Congress leader in Rajasthan at war with Chief Minister Ashok Gehlot? How do you explain that he arrogates to himself the power to decide the fate of the government in Punjab by appointing as state Congress president Navjot Sidhu, a temperamental former cricketer and former BJP member who was recently flirting with AAP, a loose cannon with doubtful loyalties, a fierce baiter of the feisty Chief Minister Capt. Amarinder Singh, thereby discommoding the latter and paving the way for the destabilisation of his own party government. The toadies continue to worship the Gandhi totem, unmindful of an imminent shipwreck.

What about the sordid affairs of Karnataka? B.S. Yediyurappa became the Chief Minister of Karnataka, illegitimately in a sense, by orchestrating the defections of Congress and JD(S) legislators and luring them into the BJP fold. He was, in turn, ousted ignominiously by his own high command instead of being removed by the elected representatives. The defections caused heartburn among both the defectors and party loyalists who were not rewarded with cabinet berths, who in all likelihood were egged on by the senior leaders of their own party to revolt. In a classic replay from the Congress's playbook, when dissidence peaked, the high command was swift in coercing Yediyurappa, a thorn in their flesh, to quit his post. Even as he sobbed and thanked those who sacked him in a tragicomedy as he resigned, he lamented that he had been hobbled by the party high command and was not allowed to form his cabinet for months even as the state was in the throes of floods and the pandemic. The new chief minister had to wait for the BJP high command to decide on his cabinet as legislators watched mutely.

The third fatal malaise that has afflicted all our political parties and the public is what Will Durant called the shameless disease of hero worship. It is good for a country to be inspired by great leaders, but they should not be blindly worshipped. They must be continually and critically evaluated. On 25 November 1949, in his last speech to the Constituent Assembly, Babasaheb Ambedkar called upon the country to work towards not only political but also social democracy and to avoid hero worship. Quoting John Stuart Mill, he urged the people not 'to lay their liberties at the feet of even a great man, or to trust him with powers which enable him to subvert their institutions'. Ambedkar went on to warn that 'Bhakti in religion may be a sure road to the salvation of the soul. But in politics, Bhakti or hero-worship is a sure road to degradation and to eventual dictatorship.'

In our impatience with institutions and dissenting opinions that are blamed for slowing the country's progress, there are temptations to emulate autocratic states like China. The worst democracy, with all its imperfections, is better than the best dictatorship. All political parties desire a vibrant democracy when it comes to state or national elections and demand free and fair elections, but they deny the same to members of their own parties. Can there be genuine democracy in the country when there is dictatorship within its political parties?

Even after he was thrown out of office by his people just months after he had led Britain through its greatest peril to victory in World War II, Winston Churchill remarked, 'Democracy is the worst form of government, except for all the others that have been tried from time to time.'

Who would know better?

*Deccan Herald*, August 2021

# For the Victors, the Vanquished and the Also-Rans

The Assembly elections in West Bengal, Assam, Kerala, Tamil Nadu and Puducherry are over, the results are out, and the governments are in place. And there are lessons for the victors, the vanquished and the also-rans.

Calling TMC leader Mamata Banerjee a Bengal tigress as she leads West Bengal for the third time is no exaggeration. An increased steadfastness despite the odds, a rare self-possession when things seem to fall apart and when allies and friends desert you, relying on your own counsel when at the crossroads, possessing a raw courage combined with perseverance and, above all, being fearless are all characteristics of valour. Ms Banerjee showed all these traits in abundance, leading from the front.

## A case for unity

Among the many lessons, there are two overriding common messages: first, that arrogance and hubris will destroy you whether you are dealing with a virulent virus or with people. Second, humanity must unite to conquer the virus. To build a happy and prosperous nation, politicians and people must come together, rising above caste, creed, gender and blinkered ideologies and pursue inclusive politics.

## Governance so far

The BJP was trounced in West Bengal, Tamil Nadu and Kerala, but it registered wins in Assam and Puducherry. It increased its seat tally in West Bengal, but seen in the blazing light of Ms Banerjee's crushing victory, any claim by the BJP to its accomplishments was invisible and immaterial. The entire focus of the world and the media was rightly on West Bengal. Many feared that a win for the BJP here would have emboldened the party leadership to pursue more vigorously its bulldozing methods of majoritarian politics, which was becoming increasingly divisive along ideological and communal lines. Enforcing its own 'Hindutva' ideology, which is antithetical to the oceanic all-embracing core Hindu philosophy, pursuing a brand of jingoistic narrow nationalism that considered anyone who disagreed as anti-national, exhibiting utter disregard for academic and press freedoms and a contempt for science while wallowing in the glories of our past accomplishments in mythology, diminishing the autonomy of institutions and investigating agencies and using them to intimidate critics and political opponents and resorting to crude moral policing that coerced people to adhere to its ideology are the factors that led to the gross vulgarization and degradation of the polity and society, which was also scarred by violence and vigilante justice. The real threat to India's vibrant democracy, its rich variegated culture and its diversity were the crude attempts to homogenize it into a depressing monochrome.

## Not inclusive

In its relentless pursuit of such politics, the party leadership, in its arrogance and hubris and blinded by power, did not realize that it was alienating a large population of its voter base, voters from across non-traditional vote banks who had switched to the BJP over the years after being disillusioned by the venal politics of the Opposition parties, both at the Centre and in the states. The politics of the BJP did not pave the way for an inclusive development model. It failed to recognize that no other model can deliver equitable growth. People eventually tire of politics that is always on the boil and that is not accommodating and reconciliatory. In the end, they want harmony, peace and freedom to pursue their faiths, professions and individual proclivities. If there is constant conflict and strife between various sections of society, no business, big or small, will thrive. Considering all these factors, the Bengal elections, in particular, were a watershed moment for the party and the country.

## Advice for the TMC leader

However, in Ms Banerjee's massive victory, there is also a lesson on defeat – a cautionary tale that should bring her down to the earth. The BJP has been steadily breaching her citadel, which began during the parliamentary elections in 2019. And she ought to be reminded that she has been no less autocratic than the BJP. She single-handedly put an end to Left Front rule of over three decades. In the process, she welcomed many lumpen elements into the TMC's fold, and the violence continued under her patronage. She was accused of nepotism within the family and favouritism in the party and for rewarding loyalty over honesty or competence. She turned a blind eye to widespread corruption and scams.

Now that she has won the mandate for a third term, she must show maturity and sagacity. She must administer through wide consultations and deliver on her promises. She can be reminded that minority appeasement vote bank politics can boomerang and give rise to a majoritarian backlash. She must not undermine and misuse the institutions and agencies of the state against her opponents and critics, a charge she often makes against the BJP. The BJP has now won seventy-seven seats in the state, which is no mean achievement. The venom and ugliness of this election must be put behind, and Ms Banerjee must work with the Opposition. If she does not heed the writing on the wall, the BJP is sure to breach the palace gates in the next elections.

## In the other States

The same lessons apply to Kerala and Tamil Nadu, too, with Pinarayi Vijayan winning a second consecutive term and M.K. Stalin making his debut as the Chief Minister of Tamil Nadu. The past tenures of the Left Democratic Front (LDF) and the DMK have not been free of controversies and scandals, high-handedness and strong-arm tactics.

Let us take a look at the Assam vote too, which, under the BJP, has been riven along communal and ethnic lines and divided on citizenship and registration rules; its citizens have had a harrowing experience. The Bengal defeat will hopefully teach the BJP that laws and rules must unite communities and the nation.

A few last words to the also-rans, especially Rahul Gandhi of the Congress party. He should be aware of what General Douglas MacArthur said: 'It is fatal to enter any war without the will to win it.'

*The Hindu*, May 2021

# Pseudo Hindus and Pseudo Seculars

Lofty words like secular, liberal and intellectual have mutated and been replaced by 'sickular', 'libtard' and 'urban naxal' and are now fashionable jargon of derision among many urban middle class. One may call them the 'Hindu bourgeois', but I'm tempted to describe them as 'Pseudo-Hindus'. They don't wear saffron, but you can see them from a mile away. Are these pseudo-Hindus a bigger threat to Hinduism today than proselytizing Christian missionaries and jihadi mullahs? Is Hinduism under siege with pseudo-Hindus leading the charge?

Before we get to that, a few words about pseudo seculars and the damage they have caused – they cannot be ignored or easily forgiven. There are quite a few of them among us, and you can spot them too without difficulty. If lofty words like secular and liberal have taken on different connotations today than what they originally meant to us, it's because 'pseudo seculars' pledged allegiance to a party and its politics and to a dead ideology above fealty to their own intelligence. They were also selective in its practice.

The pseudo seculars wished to uplift Dalits, which was noble, but condescendingly looked down upon their religious beliefs; they wanted Dalits to embrace the Leftist ideology but on the condition that they abandon their 'faith', that is, stop worshipping their village deities if they want to be emancipated. The pseudo seculars were not only contemptuous about everything traditional and cultural among the poor and lower class but were also scornful of Hindus and their belief systems, even though there is so much else to be ashamed of in our society. In the eagerness to uphold minority rights, the pseudo seculars turned blind to the terrorism of Islamic jihadis who killed Sikhs and Hindus in Kashmir that resulted in mass exodus.

The pseudo seculars did not hound them with the same zeal that they now attack the cow/gau jihadis and the crazed Hindus who are sowing seeds of hatred in India. In short, they became pompous 'secular fanatics' and created a fertile ground for majoritarian backlash.

Great liberal intellectuals like Bertrand Russell and Albert Einstein – although non-believers – had a generosity of spirit and empathy for humankind. Einstein, not a believer in a personal god who rewards and punishes human beings, said – 'I'm a deeply religious non-believer. This is a somewhat new kind of religion.'

This essay is not about politicians. They really don't care tuppence about their religious beliefs or secular ideologies. Their concerns are votes. Ronald Reagan summed it up well: 'It has been said that politics is the second oldest profession. I have learned that it bears a striking resemblance to the first.'

## The danger lies within

Now, the pseudo seculars have been largely reduced to irrelevance today. In fact, the threat to Hinduism is not so much from political parties, pseudo seculars, Indian Muslims or even imagined Islamic invaders. It's from within. The peril for Hindus in India, the society at large and for Hindus abroad is from pseudo-Hindus.

The danger to a civilization and its ethos is more when the common people in a society turn to hatred to feed their demons and fill their day purveying falsehoods. Some days you are overwhelmed with stories that shatter you, senseless communal killings and arson when lives and livelihoods are destroyed. And there is a sinking feeling, leaving many of us guilty that we didn't do enough. This is what I wish to talk about. Conflicts between various religions and wars among religious sects and ethnicities go back over 2,000 years of recorded history, but a new measles, a contagion worse than the novel coronavirus, has infected people in many parts of the world. It is more virulent in India and is corroding its very soul. Einstein said 'nationalism' is the new measles for mankind.

Not a day goes by when we don't receive messages on our social media sites and WhatsApp groups spewing venom and inflaming communal passions. One ignores it if the senders and also the messages are anonymous forwards. But when you receive communications from childhood classmates, relatives, friends and colleagues from work who you thought were easy-going, genial and loving, with whom you have broken bread over wine and loved and laughed, what do you do? When you see them blindly sending to you and twenty others some nameless person's opinion, or provocative comments and reports of incidents of prejudice full of malignant animosity, brazen falsehoods and improbable inventions of a sick mind, then you feel engulfed in despondency. When you show evidence and tell them that the audio of Lakshmi Mittal abusing Muslims in four-letter words is fake or when you tell the NRI in the United States that the anonymous viral message about Hindus becoming a minority in India by 2050 is mischievous, not backed by any evidence, and that they must not foolishly believe such things, then there's no answer. If you ask them what they mean when they say 'Hindus must rise', all you get is more fake forwards.

You feel as though there's iron in your soul. When you look at India's great sages and saints, considered the greatest of Hindus – Adi Shankaracharya, Narsi Mehta, Mirabai, M.K. Gandhi, Rabindranath Tagore, Aurobindo, Paramahansa Yogananda, Swami Vivekananda, Basavanna, Thiruvalluvar and many others – one trait runs common through all of them: they all breathed the divinity of unity through love and compassion and what one of Kannada's greatest poets Kuvempu called 'Vishwa Manava' (Universal Man).

## The shallow Hindus who can't see

And to think that the old frail Hindu who made non-violence his creed, whom Einstein likened to Jesus and Buddha, was shot dead by a fanatic Hindu. Three bullets. Point-blank range. And life extinguished. I imagined if Lord Rama, the embodiment of the noblest virtues, in whom everything desirable in a person was enshrined, if 'He' were to be walking invisibly and hear a political leader shout '*goli maaro saalon ko* (shoot the traitors)' in his name, then let alone Rama, even Ravana would have blanched and said, 'These are no Hindus. These are pseudo-Hindus.' These may be aberrations of unhinged individuals carried away by rage. But what stuns you is the indulgence and patronage they received from the senior functionaries and, more shockingly, the many 'farzi Hindus' who joined in chorus and echoed the politician's call to murder.

Is Hinduism in peril? No, not in my opinion. It has survived 3,000 years of onslaughts and alien influences. The Charavakas, a sceptical and materialistic school of philosophy, founded by Brihaspati around 600 BCE, which rejected the Vedic rituals and prevailing belief systems, were absorbed by Hinduism like a giant boa constrictor, leaving no trace of them after a few hundred years. As the Mexican poet and Nobel laureate Octavio Paz memorably wrote in *In Light of India*: 'Like an enormous metaphysical boa, Hinduism slowly and relentlessly digests foreign cultures, gods, languages and beliefs. Hinduism does not convert individuals; it absorbs communities and tribes, their gods and rites.' It appropriates and assimilates everything that comes its way. It also spawned great religions – Buddhism, Jainism and Sikhism – and allowed them to coexist and spread.

Will Hinduism morph itself into a religion of narrow outlook to compete with and resemble medieval Islamic States because of pseudo-Hindus on a rampage? That will be giving too much credit to shallow men, the 'hollow men, stuffed men, leaning together, headpiece filled with straw'.

But there's a feeling: a 'virus' is debilitating and destabilizing our society. And Hindus who believe in 'Vasudhaiva Kutumbakam' (the world is one family) must not succumb to this virus.

Something precious seems to have been lost.

William Wordsworth's famous lines from *Ode: Intimations of Immortality* come to mind:

'The glory and the freshness of a dream.
Turn wheresoe'er I may,
By night or day,
The things which I have seen I now can see no more.'

*The Print*, May 2020

# A Mandate from the Youthful Multitudes

The people have spoken in the Delhi election. So has Home Minister Amit Shah. He admitted earlier that month that provocative slogans by a few of his cabinet colleagues and party members during the campaign may have contributed to the BJP's loss. But he also wondered aloud in the same breath, 'Who knows why the people of Delhi voted the way they did.' Was this an expression of genuine remorse or a show of disappointment?

Arvind Kejriwal won handsomely. But the victory of AAP and, more pertinently, the defeat of the BJP have a message that goes much beyond the results. The election was clearly a clash of two ideologies and a contest for two visions of India. One is about fashioning India into a 'Hindu' nation in the image of the Rashtriya Swayamsevak Sangh (RSS) – the ideological fount of the BJP – an image that is distinct from the idea and ethos of India and philosophy of Hinduism as enunciated in the Upanishads and Gita and interpreted by the likes of Mahatma Gandhi, Rabindranath Tagore, Ramakrishna Paramahansa, Swami Vivekananda and many eminent philosophers of the East and the West. It is a zealous, jingoistic and parochial interpretation of Hinduism called 'Hindutva' where nationalism and patriotism are equated to a subscription to the ironclad ideology that the BJP espouses. The other vision is composed of a universal spirit, a philosophy that embraces all creation. And the latter won.

## Focus on livelihood issues

It is true that Mr Kejriwal never openly drew a sword and invited Mr Shah and Prime Minister Narendra Modi to a direct duel on the two ideologies but spoke mostly of issues pertaining to education, school, water, electricity and governance and delivery. And, in the end, the mandate was unambiguous – voters of Delhi soundly rejected Hindutva forces. While Mr Shah and his party invoked their own version of Ram and equated those with a differing, nobler idea of Ram to Pakistan sympathizers, Mr Kejriwal paid obeisance to Hanuman but without any collateral demands of loyalty. The BJP turned this election into a Hindu–Muslim, nationalism–anti-nationalism referendum instead of a governance and developmental contest. And the party's chosen, proprietary 'god' clearly failed it.

In stark contrast to the BJP's interpretation of Hinduism stands, Mahatma Gandhi, a devout and proud Hindu and, at the same time, an embodiment of love for all his fellow beings. Embracing Hinduism for the Mahatma was never in conflict with subscribing to elements of Islamic or Christian schools of thought.

True, Mr Kejriwal is no Gandhi. He is erratic and often abrasive and perennially in confrontation mode. He has been criticized by intellectuals and secularists for not visiting Shaheen Bagh, Jawaharlal Nehru University or Jamia Millia Islamia and for dodging questions on the issues of the anti-Citizenship (Amendment) Act protests and police violence in the capital. During the campaign and later, Mr Kejriwal remained astute and canny. Not crossing swords with Mr Modi or Mr Shah was a poll strategy for him. He won by controlling the narrative and, instead of playing into the hands of Mr Shah, deftly navigating the minefield the BJP was trying to draw him into and harping on the AAP's record on good governance and issues of livelihood. And it was the BJP that side-stepped these burning issues — the 'Modi mantra' that, in fact, catapulted the BJP to power in 2014.

## What influenced the voters

Yet, there is a larger pan-India message from this election. It is no longer the politicians who are steering the discourse and narrative on matters of serious import to the country. It is not the BJP that is in command now, though it succeeded through polarisation in the 2019 general elections. It is not Mr Kejriwal either, though his victory brought relief and gave some insight into where the majority community stood on communal issues and what mattered to them. And it is certainly not the Congress, which is rudderless, or the regional chieftains, none of whom has a pan-India appeal or presence. It is not the courts or the intellectuals in command. It is the youth across the country and, of late, the women who are leading the fight against communal, divisive and hateful politics and are influencing the voters today. These agitators, with their stoic courage and resilience, are demanding justice and freedom to dissent and lighting up the torch of democracy. In a role reversal, they are inspiring the celebrities, intellectuals and leaders of civil society and breathing hope and optimism where darkness and despair reigned before.

It is remarkable and laudable that these people have risen spontaneously in one voice. It seems as though, uncannily and collectively, they have understood that the Opposition is incapable of speaking up for them. They have realized that they need to stand up for themselves against the arrogance, venality and might of the state that is threatening their very future and tearing up the marvellous and cohesive social fabric that held India together. There was a Gandhi, a Bose, a Patel, a Nehru against the British; a JP Narayan to take on the dictatorship of Indira Gandhi; an Anna against the UPA's corruption and crony politics but this time around, there is no one leader leading the movement. It is as though the sea has risen.

The people of this country are now under the spell of the youth — these are intrepid young men and women from every social strata and religious and caste denomination; these are the silent women whose silent protests are more eloquent than all the fiery speeches. It is these people who have left an impression on the voters and made an impact on their voting choices. This is the answer to Mr Shah's bewildered remark at the recent summit: 'Who knows why the people of Delhi voted the way they did.'

If the politicians care to listen to the message people have sent through the mandate in the Delhi election, it is this: Don't use religion for votes. Focus on governance. Create jobs. Improve the standards of living of the people. There are enough laws and provisions in the Constitution to deal with any kind of threats to the country. The many institutions and arms of the government, both at the State and Centre, can take care of the various serious problems facing the country, including citizenship issues. Do not interfere with and influence the institutions. Don't demand allegiance to the ruling party. The people's allegiance is to the rule of law. Their fealty is to the Constitution.

The youth and women have risen and given hope to the country. If the politicians don't heed their warning and meet their demands, they will surely rein the leaders in. Their gods, then, may not be enough to hoist them to power.

*The Hindu*, February 2020

# Chidambaram's Arrest: The Hunter Becomes the Hunted

When in power, politicians feel immortal. They make laws thinking they will rule forever. The laws that they make, the police state that they create – beholden to them while they hold the reins – come back to bite them when out of power.

When intoxicated with power, it is easy to forget that the wheel of fortune forever turns and may one day run over you. It is a poignant irony that the Enforcement Directorate (ED), CBI and all the dreaded agencies which reported to P. Chidambaram – at one time or another – are now hounding him, trying to lock him up. The hunter is now the hunted.

A wistful thought may not have escaped Chidambaram and the Congress: 'If only the Congress, when in power for all those years, had made these various institutions independent of the ruling party, completely autonomous and yet accountable to a larger oversight committee, the situation may have been different.' It will haunt them for a long time.

A television anchor asked a BJP spokesperson, 'Won't people say it's too glaring and obvious that this is vendetta politics? Chidambaram, as home minister, was instrumental in getting Amit

Shah arrested and sending him to jail. Now Amit Shah is paying him back with the same coin.'

The spokesperson, grinning like a Cheshire cat, answered smugly along expected lines: 'Amit Shah or the government has nothing to do with it. The CBI is independent. The law has to take its course. Nobody is above the law.'

Congress leaders, equally glib, were at pains to convince everyone that 'this was an attempt to silence the opposition, an assault on democracy. Amit Shah was using CBI as his private detective agency, and the agencies were riding roughshod on the fundamental rights of individuals'.

## The CBI's autonomy

Can anyone overlook the 'caged parrot' epithet that was earned by the CBI during the Congress's rule? The agencies were at the beck and call of the ruling parties, ready to do their bidding and rein in the Opposition leaders who were politically inconvenient to the ruling dispensation. The Damocles sword of the CBI was always hanging over their heads, to be used at will, perennially keeping corruption and criminal cases on the Opposition leaders hanging, which were deliberately never closed for decades. The Congress never had any qualms in unleashing an investigating agency to secure political support from the Opposition leaders at critical junctures.

There may be consternation, despair and even wringing of hands in the Congress camp for not doing what they should have and could have easily done when Anna Hazare laid siege to Delhi. He demanded that the UPA II government under Manmohan Singh appoint a Lokpal and bring the CBI under its purview to make it autonomous.

On the other side of the divide, there may be sadistic glee and justification among the BJP's followers that Chidambaram needs no empathy.

The issue is not about Shah or Chidambaram but about the misuse of executive power. It is about the autonomy and sanctity of various institutions, not just the CBI or ED, but others such as the law department and the offices of the attorney and solicitor generals. Under duress, their allegiance has not always been to justice and the rule of law. It cannot be to any particular party or an individual who exercises power – ministers, bureaucrats – but to an overarching fidelity to the Constitution. There can be no two opinions on that.

## Demands made by Anna Hazare

There is also the urgent need for autonomy of similar key institutions, even at the state level. This was another of Anna Hazare's demands. Though he seemed naive and rustic, he was very shrewd and perceptive. He repeatedly emphasised he was not demanding Manmohan Singh's resignation or the downfall of the UPA. He wanted systemic changes. Without that, a change of government would be a meaningless exercise. His experience had taught him over the years that successive governments were only more corrupt and more autocratic. Political parties had only one aim – to concentrate power around themselves, placing them beyond the pale of law.

Indeed, in the present case, there are definite and troubling questions about the legal niceties and, as some would say, the crude handling of the arrest. As a former CBI director told a television channel, 'The agency could have shown more sensitivity and finesse.' They need not have gone about this circus of scaling walls and jumping fences under the public glare of television cameras as though they were apprehending an armed terrorist.

That overzealous show of bravado – where no enemy fire or danger lurked – was comic and reminded one of Tom Sawyer's adventures. This tamasha of sorts was voyeuristic entertainment during the evening staple of television news. It was an adrenalin-bursting release for television anchors. It was the humiliation of a former home minister, his family and friends and of the Grand Old Party. But for many in the saffron party and its sympathizers, it may have been a primaeval urge, a gladiatorial bloodletting to avenge a past.

## Reshaping institutions

If all these tumultuous events and their nature can serve any public good, it is that the focus must shift to the necessity of reforms to bring autonomy and credibility to many of our institutions.

Even if the CBI and ED had acted independently and justly in Chidambaram's case, their actions are always suspect. These institutions are organizationally structured to be controlled by the party in power. If their autonomy is not ensured by statute – with adequate checks and balance – and if they are not seen to be outside the clutches of the ruling parties, their credibility will always be under a cloud, their motives always questioned. This will affect the morale and efficiency of the agencies. No one can be expected to discharge their duties to their full potential if they are not held in high esteem. There cannot be any trust deficit between the general public and these institutions.

There may be a moral to the story in all this. As someone said, 'Politicians who make laws must now and then live under those laws.' It will chasten them and will also be good for society.

*The Wire*, August 2019

# Ayodhya Verdict and the Rashomon Effect

The incidents leading up to the recent Ayodhya verdict by the Supreme Court of India and subsequent reactions reminded me of Akira Kurosawa's much-acclaimed film *Rashomon*. In that extraordinary movie, the wife of a samurai is raped by a notorious bandit in a forest. The husband, who is tied up by the bandit, watches the horrific act. After the rape, the bandit, failing to convince the wife to marry him, challenges the samurai to a duel and kills him. A woodcutter, collecting wood nearby, witnesses the rape and the killing. The stories narrated by the four witnesses, including the dead husband, and told through a 'medium', are varying, conflicting, contradictory, confusing and seem motivated by self-interest and coloured by ego and attempts to save face. The Ayodhya verdict and the subsequent flood of widely differing opinions and reactions in print and electronic media, the infinite variety of comments on social media and the cacophony of multiple voices on television channels by scores of opinion makers, much like the film *Rashomon*, depict multiple realities, revealing the difficulty of understanding past events presented by subjectivity of truth and uncertainty of factual realities. While there are four different narratives of the same event in the film by four witnesses, in the Ayodhya case, there were innumerable actors with a multitude of opinions with contrasting shades and versions and interpretations. History, mythology, fact, faith, belief, religion, rituals, politics, communal tension, vested interests, greed for land, traditions and the law, letter and spirit of the constitution all co-mingled and left varying impressions on the numerous actors. The religious leaders, political parties, affiliates of political parties like the RSS, Vishva Hindu Parishad (VHP), All India Muslim Personal Law Board, Sunni Waqf Board, many Ram Janmabhoomi associated trusts, various extremists and fringe elements, warring parties who are parties to the suit on both sides of the divide, public at large, bureaucrats and government brought to bear their influence on the judges, who are only all too human.

In such complex and ambiguous situations, myriad events from a hoary past are effaced and altered and superimposed with fresh images and writings and, as in a palimpsest, are contested. Disagreements leading to sectarian violence go back 150 years and remain unresolved through litigations and mediations. In such cases, the Supreme Court bench comprising five judges, who can also never be completely free of subjective and objective perceptions, gives a unanimous decision after sifting through thousands of pages of arguments and evidence and after hearing hundreds of witnesses and lawyers. Such a judgement is a miracle in itself and must be hailed and welcomed. One could argue that there could have been different options leading to other kinds of judgements. The Supreme Court had to choose an ideologically neutral option from the various choices before it. An easy escape route would have been to 'not decide' by evading a seemingly intractable, complex and sensitive case such as this and to keep postponing through prevarication, as was done over the previous seventy years. The provincial administrations before Independence during the British rule also allowed this to simmer and fester. Based on available evidence that possession of parts of the disputed site was jointly held by the Muslims and Hindus for many decades and bearing in mind that the dispute originated in 1850 and that the mosque was built 450 years ago on ancient temple ruins with no proof that it was destroyed for building the mosque, but taking into account the belief of the Hindus since time immemorial that Rama, a sacred deity, was born there but unable to legally determine the title of the land in favour of either party, the judges could have delivered a cussed judgement and ousted both parties and allotted alternate lands to both and sealed up the land forever. That would have been another Molotov cocktail left unattended while the fire was still unextinguished. There could have been other options for a final verdict. But the judges, in their wisdom, going by assurances from all parties that they would respect and abide by the verdict regardless of which way it went, opted to put a final closure on the dispute. In a typical ancient method practiced by the panchayat system, which resolves a dispute between warring parties by taking into account not only legal factors but emotions and all angles and aspects of the dispute, the five judges delivered a verdict, allotting the disputed site where the Babri Masjid once stood to the Hindus and an alternate site of five acres in a prominent place in Ayodhya to the Muslims, leaving it to the magnanimity and prudence of the government to allot the specific site for building a new masjid. The Court could perhaps have allotted the alternate site within the sixty-seven acres acquired by the government where once the Babri was located, where the idols of Rama are also kept, and put a lid on the matter instead of leaving that part open. But the judges may have had their own reasons to leave that discretion to the government. It was time to put out the fire and end the fight once and for all.

Already there are voices of protest and criticism and expressions of disappointment on the judgement from the Muslim bodies and spokespersons. The parties to the dispute from the Muslim side are also not in agreement on their future action plan and are yet to decide their way forward. A few have said they are not in favour of a review petition. The various sections of the Hindus are not aligned on how the temple will be run or who should be on the proposed government trust. The numerous Hindu religious orders, sadhus and saints representing the many religious outfits fighting for a Rama temple in Ayodhya, along with the larger, well-known national bodies like the VHP and RSS, while unanimously welcoming the verdict, have already frenetically begun lobbying, trying to find a voice and place for themselves in the government-appointed trust responsible for the construction and management of the temple. All these are not uncommon. Such a role for oneself is, after all, all about influence, power and money, as the Rama temple will attract millions of Hindus. It will be, according to many, as important a pilgrimage site as Kashi. The Muslims who put up a fight for retaining the disputed site where the Babri Masjid once stood have to come to terms and decide on the new masjid – its location, construction and management. It will attract millions of their faith and can also be a tourist attraction by the sheer drama and history behind its construction. But many are still undecided and divided on their next steps. Will they file a review petition? Will they continue the fight by different means? All these disagreements on both sides are normal and not unexpected. Many temple trusts, religious bodies and mutts, ashrams and cults of godmen, waqfs, churches and missionary denominations have often been in bitter disputes over control of the trusts and their properties and funds. They have gone to court over the way they are managed and run. The devotees, divided on sectarian lines, have even contested the forms of worship, text of chants or symbols used on the deity's forehead, as was the case between the warring priests of the Tirupati temple, which is still not resolved to satisfaction.

The many trusts claiming to represent Ram Lalla may one day fight in the future over the management and control of the proposed Ayodhya temple, but today the large, amorphous, devout Hindus across the country are happy. The various Muslim bodies may be peeved that the judgement was not fair, but it is heartening that they have affirmed that they will respect the judgement and have appealed for peace. The common Muslim may not be joyous but is heaving a sigh of relief that there is a chance now for communal harmony and they can get along with their life.

So we can sing joyously with Robert Browning:

The lark's on the wing;
The snail's on the thorn;
God's in his heaven –
All's right with the world!

*The Times of India*, November 2019

# Narendra Modi: Statesman or Pretender?

It is said that while a politician thinks of the next election, a statesman thinks of the next generation. The reactions to Modi's repeal of the farm laws are divided along predictable lines. Modi's ardent fans and his senior party members and spokespersons, always taking a cue from his pronouncements, who were until recently heaping abuse on the protesting farmers, calling them anti-nationals, have hailed Modi's decision. Home Minister Amit Shah tweeted that by revoking the farm laws, 'Modi has shown remarkable statesmanship.' Those from the Opposition termed his move as a climbdown. P. Chidambaram, the Congress leader and former finance minister, said, 'PM Modi was not inspired by policy or change of heart but was impelled by fear of elections!'

Apolitical analysts, including many from the foreign media, have observed that his decision to cancel the farm laws, though late, was a way to reverse the political slide the BJP had experienced in the recent by-elections and to regain lost ground. John Elliot, the former New Delhi bureau chief of the *Financial Times*, says Modi caved in apprehending a setback in the forthcoming state elections, especially in Uttar Pradesh, which would have an important bearing on the national elections in 2024. It has dented Modi's strongman image.

The sudden announcement of the repeal of the three farm laws took the nation by surprise. However, no one is astonished at Modi's characteristic way of catching you off guard. The overnight demonetization of higher denomination currency notes five years ago shocked the nation, sending the growing economy into a tailspin. When the pandemic struck, he announced a nationwide lockdown with just a few hours' notice, without preparation or dialogue with the states who had to implement the lockdown, resulting in the largest mass movement of people – migrant labourers – across India since Partition, causing chaos and panic and freezing supply chains of essentials. And last year, he imposed the farm laws without consultations with the various stakeholders, ramming them through an Ordinance first and later rushing them into laws without debate in Parliament.

Now, the rescinding of the farm laws has startled everyone – farmers and politicians alike. Though it was increasingly becoming clear to everyone that the farm laws had eroded the voter base of the BJP by alienating and angering farmers in the states of Uttar Pradesh, Punjab and Haryana, most people, going by his past actions, thought Modi wouldn't buckle. Indeed, it appeared so for many months, even as the farmers dug in and defied him. Modi's political confidantes were emboldened and opted for a strategy of wearing out the farmers while simultaneously attempting to divide them, assuming that the protests would dissipate.

Modi did not defer to either the opposition parties to elicit their views and accommodate them or consult agricultural economists across the spectrum or even confer with his own cabinet colleagues. He chose to rely on his own counsel, as is his wont.

He was, in a sense, well served by a few of his earlier unilateral actions. Though the economy may have tanked as a consequence of nullifying 86 per cent of cash from the economy overnight through demonetization, without any visible gains, curiously, he benefited immensely politically. To the dismay of his opponents and amazement of poll pundits, contrary to their predictions and hopes, he led the BJP to a landslide victory in the 2017 UP elections. The masses, who had never seen a ₹1,000 note, truly believed that Modi was slaying the invisible demons of black money, which the rich supposedly hoarded in cash in high-value currency notes, though there was no evidence to support this.

The migrants, small-scale businesses and industry suffered due to his forced lockdown, too, but even that did not dent his image. He swiftly realized (though he has neither admitted nor apologized for it) that the lockdown was a hare-brained idea, and, when the second COVID-19 wave hit the country, he wisely decentralized and transferred the management of the pandemic to the states, including even the procurement of vaccines at a time when they were about to hit a shortage, only to take back the responsibility just as vaccine production picked up. And fortune smiled on him. The pandemic waned. His detractors continued their attack on him, but it did not stick with the public, who forgave everything – the serious lapses of oxygen shortage, shortage of vaccines and ICU beds and ventilators when the Covid virus raged and killed millions.

All these probably gave Modi a sense of invincibility. Who can be beyond it? Our mythology is full of legends of even sages and rishis who, through their austere penance, acquired formidable power and became arrogant. The jealous gods had to then send the likes of the bewitching Menaka to destroy the arrogance of the likes of Vishwamitra.

Emperor Napoleon, who lived and conquered by the sword and was defeated by it in the end, said that 'morale and opinion are more than half the battle'. Modi failed to read the opinion and spirit of the farmers. He underestimated their morale and their stoic courage and perseverance to continue their struggle despite overwhelming odds. Power clouds the vision, and courtiers screen one from reality. Any people's movement that can sustain for a year will win in the end. This is the same blunder that the Manmohan Singh government and Congress made in dealing with the Anna Hazare-led India Against Corruption movement when he laid siege to Delhi.

A statesman's head must reside in his heart. This is a good lesson for Modi and for the leaders of all political parties. No one can disagree that the agriculture sector needs far-reaching reforms. But reforms, to be successful, require conciliation, consensus, cooperation and patience.

Edmund Burke said, 'The great difference between the real statesman and the pretender is that the one sees into the future while the other regards only the present.' Whether Modi is a statesman or a mere pretender is the province of future historians when they view him years from now – time will lend a better perspective.

For now, his decision to repeal the farm laws and his 'apology' to the nation and the announcement that he will constitute a committee that will involve all stakeholders, including state governments, farmers and agriculture scientists and economists, are welcome and eminently sensible.

*Deccan Herald*, November 2021

# Kashi Corridor: Highway of Faith or Narrow Lane of Communal Politics?

When Prime Minister Narendra Modi inaugurated the grand corridor to the Kashi Viswanath temple on 13 December 2021, nostalgia swept over me. The earliest, from my childhood in the mid-1950s, is of an enterprising Vadyar – a Sri Vaishnava priest – who organized an annual pilgrimage tour by hiring a bus, complete with provisions, cooks and utensils, to visit the holiest of the holy temples of India, from Tirupati to Kashi and Badrinath in the Himalayas. He arranged night halts in dharmshalas, was fluent in Sanskrit and Hindi, knew the rules of these temples, was well-versed in the Puranas and scriptures and enthralled the pilgrims with legends and lore associated with the deities and the mythic rivers over the forty-five days of the tour. The Kashi Viswanath darshan and Ganga snan were the high points of the tour. It dawned on me very early the inscrutable hold they had and the centrality of Kashi and Ganga on the lives, sentiments and imagination of Hindus, especially on Vadyar's perennial stream of Brahmin pilgrims.

Later, in my twenties, when I first boarded an Indian Airlines flight, the notes of shehnai that wafted through the plane as I entered the cabin captivated me, and it has remained a haunting melody since. And that lilting, soul-seeping tune by Ustad Bismillah Khan is, to me, inextricably linked to the Kashi Viswanath temple. The words of the Ustad, a devout Muslim who said that his music was a gift from Lord Vishwanath, still resonate in my mind.

The third imagery associated with the Ganga is from the heart-stirring song '*Ganga beheti hi kyon*' by Bhupen Hazarika. Bhupen laments, 'On your mighty banks, that are home to countless people, despite hearing their anguished cries, O Ganga, how do you – how can you – flow so meekly, silently and unmindfully.' He beseeches, 'Morality is destroyed and humanity is corrupted, yet shamelessly, why do you flow? … O stream of Ganga, yet why do you not turn weak into strong warriors? O Ganga, why do you keep silent?'

The song was poignant, and made you wonder, what was the point of all this worship, this 'holy dip', this seeking of personal salvation, if they did not cleanse and uplift our society and polity collectively?

The glittering inauguration of the Kashi corridor by Modi elicited responses from many quarters along the expected lines. Those from the BJP were mesmerized by the grandeur of the ceremony. The believing Hindus were moved to tears of ecstasy by the Vedic chants from the high priests. The intellectuals felt it was gross theatrical extravaganza and the height of narcissism of one man who turned the deeply pious ceremony into a marketing event, divesting it of its religious significance. Politicians were stunned by the sheer audacity of the Prime Minister, who strode through as if he were an emperor. They accused him of using religion for politics with an eye on the forthcoming UP elections.

Some asked if he should not have made the occasion a national event by inviting the Opposition parties and the heads of all religions, thereby mirroring to the world the all-embracing ethos of Hinduism. Was that not the resounding message of Swami Vivekananda when he addressed the Parliament of Religions in Chicago in 1893, where he said, 'I am proud to belong to a religion that has taught the world both tolerance and universal acceptance … We accept all religions as true. I am proud to belong to a nation which has sheltered the persecuted and the refugees of all religions and all nations of the earth.'

By turning the ceremonials into a Hindu hegemonic celebration, did it diminish a great religion and its universal appeal, which has drawn people from around the world over millennia for its spirit of enquiry, its quest for truth that sees the Creator in everything, into a parochial revelry? Power is the mistress of all politicians. The Opposition politicians wear secularism on their sleeves; the BJP politicians wear Hindutva on their robes, one to appease the minorities, the other to appease the majority community, to gain power. How are they any different? When the BJP paints the Opposition as 'anti-Hindu', they panic and start visiting Hindu temples or reciting holy chants to stop alienating Hindus. They are falling into the trap laid by the BJP. They cannot win that communal contest. Their hypocrisy and want of convictions show easily. No one knows what they stand for. At least people know what the BJP represents.

Rahul Gandhi's recent religious polemic against the Hindutva ideology of the BJP and RSS, as opposed to the Hinduism that he stands for, is a valid and much-needed debate in these toxic times. Yet, why is Rahul Gandhi not taken seriously? Why is Kejriwal, who trounced the BJP and Congress in the Delhi elections twice by unprecedented margins solely on the twin planks of governance and development, grovelling before voters, chanting mantras and promising pilgrimages? Why is he losing confidence in what he believes in?

Politicians like Nehru, Sardar Patel, Jaya Prakash Narayan and Ram Manohar Lohia needed no validation from others about their ideologies or religious beliefs nor stooped to prove that they were ardent Hindus. Their faith in humanism, fraternity and equality for all did not waver. The Opposition must ponder deeply and get their ideology and politics right.

Modi invoked the noble qualities of Rama and ideals of Ram Rajya in Ayodhya and paid obeisance to Viswanath in Kashi, with an oblique reference to those invaders like Aurangzeb who desecrated Hindu temples centuries ago. His followers took it as a call for a crusade of war against the minorities, unleashing terror and violence. The open calls for ethnic cleansing by some are the very antithesis of every ideal those deities symbolize. Modi can, and must, put a stop to this hate and violence before it gets out of hand. As he enjoys a huge mandate, his actions, his words, as well his silences, can unleash destructive forces. They can also douse the fire of hatred and heal and unite the country.

Modi can leave a legacy of bringing a sense of pride to Hindus, 'with malice toward none, with charity for all'. It may also be more prudent politics in the long run. The Hindus are amorphous and detest straight-jacketing into rigid belief systems.

Modi can mix religion with politics if he believes in the ideals and precepts of Gandhi, whom he often invokes. Gandhi, the greatest Hindu that ever lived, said, 'Those who believe religion and politics aren't connected don't understand either … For me, humanitarian service, or rather service of all that lives, is religion. And I draw no distinction between such religion and politics.'

*Deccan Herald*, January 2022

# MUSINGS

# Annadata Sukhi Bhava: Sardars of Generosity

The recurring images of our stoic farmers, who are protesting on the outskirts of Delhi, and the stout Sikhs sharing their steaming hot langar food with the hungry cops on duty are a heart-warming sight. They brought back a flood of lingering memories from my immemorial past, of two occasions out of many, when I was treated to an unexpected hearty meal. An abiding generosity of spirit, an endearing, embracing hospitality that distinguishes the jovial Sikhs in particular and the farming community in general, are in stark contrast to city folks who often shrink from opening their arms and are discommoded when guests, especially our country cousins, drop in unannounced.

Let me recount two stirring stories that capture the foregoing.

In 1972, I was posted at an observation post at Cho La, a rocky promontory at 15,000 feet above sea level, facing the Chinese outposts on the Tibetan borders, snowbound most of the year. During my tenure, I was deputed to a large contingent of forty-eight soldiers for a long-range Patrol lasting twenty-eight days. The high-altitude mission crossing 21,000 feet was to survey the infiltration routes of the Chinese from Tibetan passes and suggest remedial action. We had to be fully self-contained for the reconnaissance for eight days at a stretch and replenish ourselves at chosen border posts along the route.

After twelve days, on our return trek, it started to rain heavily. As we descended along a stream, it began to swell swiftly, fed by countless rivulets, and soon was in spate. The small bridge where we were to cross as per our map had got washed away. It was nearing dusk, and we had to quickly find a safe place to camp overnight. We were drenched to our bones. Fortunately, we had a courageous and very experienced infantry officer who took charge and led us. After an hour of slow trekking over slippery slopes, he sighted a meadow under an inch of water, where we decided to rest for the night. We took out our dwindling crumbs and ate what we could, and, huddling together in full gear in our boots, we lay down. We were so exhausted that we slept soundly even as the rains beat down on us.

Next morning, the downpour continued. We started on hungry stomachs alongside the flooded stream, believing it would lead us to some settlement. On many stretches, we had to hack our way through the undergrowth with machetes. The path was arduous with steep gorges, and as we trekked down the rocky riverbanks, there was no let-up in the rains. At one point, as we slowly trudged along the river, there was a sudden explosive sound. We were caught unawares as rocks rumbled down. Luckily, only two soldiers were injured. We marched on and took shelter before sundown. The rains lashed us.

On the third day, we started early. The rains were petering out. With no radio communication, no maps and no idea where we were, we banded together and trundled down. Around eleven in the morning, the rains abated. And suddenly, as we walked down the hills, the clouds lifted, and below us, the verdant valley revealed herself, bathed in effulgent sunlight. And we detected a swirl of smoke deep below in the valley. Life, fire, warmth! Oh, we let out a collective scream of joy.

We hurried down the mountains, and as we neared the camp around noon, a burly, jolly Sardar with a few men tagging behind him greeted us as we approached. After we introduced ourselves, he told us he was from the Intelligence Bureau and headed that outpost. We told him we had not eaten for two days. We were soaked to our soul and had tired limbs. He organized hot water for us to bathe and ordered food to be cooked.

The Sikh officer toasted us to Hercules rum, regaled us with bawdy stories and served us hot dal, chawal, roti and chicken curry. It was an unforgettable feast, fit for a king.

Many years later, after retirement from the army, when I became a farmer, I was travelling on my Enfield motorcycle with my wife and three-year-old daughter from Hassan town to my farm, a distance of fifty kilometres. Suddenly, I had a flat tyre in the middle of nowhere. It was noon, and I realized we were some ten kilometres from the nearest town where we could get the tyre fixed. Then, I saw a lone farmer in a field tucked in a mango orchard. Noticing that I was in distress, he walked towards me. On seeing I had my wife and kid and observing the flat tyre, without a moment of hesitation, he put us at ease with his disarming smile and led us to his house and introduced us to his wife. He then gave me his tractor and a farmhand to ferry the bike to the town for repair and assured me that my wife and kid could relax in the meantime. I returned by two in the afternoon, ravenously hungry. I profusely thanked him and wished to take his leave. He said it was lunchtime, and he would not let us leave without sharing the meal with his family. It was such a delicious ploughman's repast that it surpassed any banquet for the potentates.

When you are lost and famished and are invited by a generous and genial Sardar to break bread over wine or by a farmer to join in the family lunch, a humble meal offered by the affable host has no equal.

And now, when I see the earthy farmers sitting in protest on the borders of Delhi, forsaken and forlorn, those denizens of our rural heartland who tirelessly till and toil on their lands to feed us all year, my heart aches and goes out in prayer for them, for an early resolution. The government must show magnanimity and prudence and climb down from the pedestal to break the deadlock and enable them to return with dignity to their home and hearth and their lands, to keep us well provided.

*Annadata Sukhi Bhava*.

Are we not bound and beholden to keep those who feed us happy?

*Deccan Herald*, January 2021

# The Land of Rumi Lies in Ruins

'O Kabuliwala! Kabuliwala!' These words of Mini, the little girl in Rabindranath Tagore's short story *Kabuliwala*, still chime like jingles whenever I see Afghans or read about Afghanistan, the land of remote, forbidding and mystic mountains, the land of valiant, ancient warriors. Abdur Rahman, the tall, loose-robed, long-limbed, high-turbaned and bearded vendor of fruits and wares, who plied his goods in the back lanes of Calcutta, like many of his countrymen across many cities of India, and made his annual pilgrimage back to the land high in the mountains, has been made immortal in his Tagore's story.

Migrants are feared as aliens and seen with suspicion and antipathy, but Tagore etched the character of Kabuliwala as a kindred spirit with such delicacy, beauty and endearment that your heart swells as you read the story.

The friendship between little Mini, her father, who is an author, and Kabuliwala blossoms. But Kabuliwala is imprisoned over a stabbing incident with a buyer who owed him a debt and is put away for eight years. After his release from jail, he goes to meet Mini. It happens to be her wedding day. He is dissuaded from meeting her by the father, who thinks he could be a bad omen on the auspicious day.

When Kabuliwala offers some dry fruits as a present to Mini and turns away, deeply disappointed to depart, Mini's father, touched to the quick, asks Mini to be brought in. Kabuliwala is flustered as Mini doesn't recognize him when he tries to speak to her as he would before. She is now a bashful bride, no longer the carefree child he once knew, and she blushes and bends her head. Kabuliwala, overcome with a flood of emotions, pulls up his vest and reveals the inked imprint of the hand of his little daughter in Afghanistan and fondly runs his hand over it. Mini's father, tears in his eyes, feels they are all universally bound by the same filial bonds, offers the proud Kabuliwala some money and urges him to go back home to his own daughter, who has also now grown up. The ink-smeared impression of the hand of Kabuliwala's little Parvati in her distant home reminds him of his own little Mini. Mini's father forgets that Kabuliwala is a poor dry fruit seller from Kabul. Was he more than 'him'? He was also a father.

These heart-warming memories of the story of Kabuliwala swept over me as I saw the disturbing imagery of the fall of Kabul to the marching gangs of the Taliban fighters, rifles slung across their shoulders. Thousands of Afghan civilians, women in burkhas and hijabs, with children in arms, stricken with fear and panic, were fleeing their homes to cross the land borders to the neighbouring countries. The chaotic scenes of desperate hordes of people rushing to the airport to catch American rescue flights, apprehensive of the Taliban rule in the offing that had terrorized the population for five years in the late 1990s, clinging on to the planes in despair even as they taxied toward take-off, a few of them soon falling to their deaths as the planes were airborne, were horrifying and heartbreaking.

A land that has been ravaged over the centuries by many waves of occupational armies – from the time of Alexander the Great to the Mauryas of Magadha, the Mongols, Arab Muslims, the British, the Soviets and finally the mighty US military in 2001, along with NATO forces – the land of Rumi was 'freed' once again a few days ago by the Taliban. This is a land that is termed unconquerable and often referred to as the 'graveyard of empires'. This land, whose soil has been fertilized with the blood of millions of its people as well as irrigated by the gore of invaders over millennia, has also been the breeding ground and source from which the Greco-Bactrians, the Kushans, the Ghaznis and Ghoris, the Khiljis, the Mughals and others invaded and marauded and went on to found new empires, including in India.

While the Taliban must be condemned and reviled for spawning terrorism, despised for their bestiality in enforcing extreme Sharia law, hated for treating women abominably and loathed for ruthlessly killing innocents, and while nothing can justify any of that, were not the war games of the superpowers turned into video games of mindless killing, inflicting collateral damage on a large number of innocent women and children and civilians, especially in the rural areas, reminding one of Shakespeare's line 'as flies to wanton boys are we to the Gods; they kill us for their sport'? But above all, we have to pay homage to the common people for braving the onslaught of terrible hardships and bereavement of loved ones, and to their inextinguishable spirit and stoic courage, caught perennially as they are between the cross-currents of international geopolitics and their local tribal leaders, warlords and religious fundamentalists.

Now, the United States has abandoned the country shamelessly, leaving it in total disarray and chaos, a result of a gross disconnect between inept policy, confusing diplomacy and failure of intelligence. The Taliban, now virtually in command, is sending signals of its intention to form an inclusive government, giving a call for amnesty to everyone and promising more freedom for women to work and go to schools and colleges. But there are already reports of reprisals and killings. Analysts are divided about the genuineness or otherwise of the 'new' Taliban. The people, especially women, await in fear and foreboding.

It is a cruel irony. Jalāl ad-Dīn Muḥammad Rūmī, a twelfth-century Afghan mystic, one of the most beloved Sufi poets, a precious gift to the world, whose poems of love and peace and harmony are still heard in churches, synagogues, monasteries and temples, rose like fragrant incense from the same land that now lies in tatters, riven by bigotry and sectarian violence, torn between the imperialism of the superpowers of the world. The time has come for them to exit Afghanistan. China trying to fill the void left by the Americans and wooing the Taliban is foolhardy, and it may find its soldiers' bones interred with the graveyards of former invaders. Fools always rush in where angels fear to tread. And Pakistan forgets that one cannot export terrorism without also importing it into its own society.

And alas, India, the land of Gandhi and Buddha, seems to be out of the picture in playing a role to rebuild and bring back peace to the country with which we have historic connections and roots.

The Taliban, one hopes, will begin to build bridges. Who could have sung it better than Rumi: 'Love is the bridge between you and everything.'

*Deccan Herald*, August 2021

# R.K. Laxman the King of Cartoons and I

When Air Deccan became a popular airline and was seen as an airline of the common man with its catchline 'Every Indian Can Fly', my head of marketing, John Kuruvilla, said, 'Capt. We must find a brand ambassador for Air Deccan.' So we had a brainstorming session along with Thomas Xavier, head of our creative agency Orchard from Leo Burnett. Suggestions flew thick and fast. Some suggested a Bollywood star – Amitabh, Shahrukh, Salman, Aamir – others a sports star. And a few said I could be the brand ambassador myself in the fashion of some corporate company founders. None of this gelled, in my opinion. I felt that, though it would be good for our ego to have a Bollywood star, it went against the ethos and low-cost image of Air Deccan as a common man's airline. Besides, it would send the ad budget through the roof, rendering it disproportionate to the incremental income such a brand ambassador might generate and in turn would push the fares north, reducing occupancy. And projecting myself smacked of hubris and pomposity.

When this was agitating my mind, a brilliant cartoon by R.K. Laxman in *The Times of India* caught my attention. It was a few months after Air Deccan introduced ₹1 and ₹500 air tickets, which had created a huge buzz and captured the imagination of the country and had triggered an implosion. People from the lower strata of society had begun to experience air travel. The combination of low fares and linkage of rural towns with metros had an explosive impact and ushered in an air travel revolution overnight. The cartoon depicted a villager sitting on a flight seat expansively in smug arrogance, wrapped in a kambal, one leg on the seat, with his rural 'bistar and bedding' in the baggage cabin overhead, a water jug on the floor, known commonly as a 'rail chombu' as it was always carried by train passengers (Laxman was such a keen observer he had missed nothing). There was also a common man sitting at the window with his perennially bemused expression and a guy in a suit hemmed in the middle seat with an expression of snobbish disdain. It was such a small pocket cartoon, but the expressions were vividly etched by Laxman's lines. The man in the suit tells the common man, 'If these airlines reduce their fares any further, I will start travelling by train.' I burst out laughing. That was the cartoon of a genius. At that time, it hit me – Laxman's Common Man could be my brand ambassador and mascot. That picture would be better than a thousand ads in breaking the barrier to air travel and convey that air travel was affordable to common people and help create a tectonic consumer shift.

My marketing chief John said, 'Capt. Don't even dream of it. Laxman will bang the phone on you. We tried it in our previous company and tried to influence him through someone in the PMO. And Laxman snubbed and snapped the connection.'

I called Laxman. I said 'Namaskara' and spoke in Kannada. I was aware he had lived in Mysore. Laxman warmed up to my Kannada. We chatted freely. He loved talking to me in colloquial Kannada. I mentioned the cartoon of the villager travelling on an aeroplane. He laughed heartily. He loved poking fun at pompous, snobbish prigs. He asked me where I was from. I said a small village called Gorur near a remote rural district called Hassan. What he said next surprised me. He said his father was the headmaster in the government high school at Hassan. He had studied there. That bowled me over I later discovered Laxman's father was my father's headmaster!

I came to the point. I said I wanted to meet him. I wished to take his permission to use the Common Man on my planes as a mascot. He asked me to come to his house in Bombay.

After a week or so, I met him at his house in Bombay. What struck me first was the very middle-class ambience of his house. There was an indefinably homely feeling to it. There were many cartoons of crows hung on walls, and I learnt that that was his favourite bird. The crows looked as though they were perched on the wall, ready to take flight or move in their peculiar, funny gait. Then I saw one interesting cartoon of a young boy, seated in the middle of a room, a slate in hand, surrounded by piles of books, totally hassled and overwhelmed with all the books and subjects. The jumble of arithmetic numbers and science figures from the school textbooks that were in his head whirled like the atoms in orbit, captured lucidly in a halo around his head. There were no subtitles or text below. Just the picture of the schoolboy. I looked at it amused and with interest. He guessed and said, 'That's my son. My wife was trying to tutor him, and when she left the room, that is what I saw. The poor chap!'

I asked him if his son also drew. Quick came a retort: 'Yes.' Then a long pause. 'He draws money from the bank.' His wife Kamala was around. We all laughed. He had a sharp wit, quick repartee and a quicker temper. He did not suffer phoneys, pompous fools or cant (typically moral, religious or political) when he was face to face with such people. He did not pull his punch and spoke his mind. But how do you hit them or expose them to millions of people? He found the most effective way – through his satire and spoof in his cartoons. That one cartoon in *The Times of India* captured the essence of India's humbug and phoney politicians more effectively than all the articles on the edit page – when a minister, back from a foreign trip, alights from his plane and declares gleefully, smiling from ear to ear, that his trip abroad was a failure and he has to go back again!

We went to his study. This was the study in which, over the last few years, after he had suffered a mild stroke, he had been drawing his daily 'You Said It' cartoon. I looked at the frail man and wondered at his energy at eighty-four. For sixty years, come what may, Laxman had produced one cartoon every day of his life. How fecund! what an amazing fount of creativity! Who or what was his muse!

I broached the topic. He had, of course, heard of Air Deccan. His cartoon was a result of that. He had travelled Air Deccan. I said I wanted him to give me three fresh drawings of his Common Man that I could use as my mascot next to the Airbus door in life-size and also in our promotions and ads. I had taken a model Airbus on which my marketing team had created a replica of his Common Man as a sample. He ran his fingers over the bald, bespectacled common man as though he were a living being and, in a dreamy trance, kept touching it. Then finally, he said, 'You can use it.' He would draw three originals and present them to me. I was touched and elated. I asked him about the commercial terms. He said without batting an eyelid: 'Whatever pleases you.' I was dumbfounded.

My chief financial officer had asked me to check if there were copyright issues with *The Times of India*. I ventured gingerly to ask, for fear of offending him. He said nobody had a right over his Common Man. But, of course, the published cartoons were property of the newspaper. I couldn't use them. I pressed further, 'What if *TOI* objects!' He was at his irreverent best and retorted like a rifle shot. Laced with a Kannada expletive, he shot out, 'Will ask them to buzz off!' And exploded laughing!

Laxman's Common Man was a perfect mascot for Air Deccan. The people loved it. He was everybody's uncle and could be from any state of India. When I asked Laxman how he had decided on this image and how he had arrived at the present figure, he told me this: in the first few years, the Common Man differed every day depending on the context and situation. You could make out that he was a common man but also discern that he hailed from Tamil Nadu or Karnataka or Maharashtra or West Bengal. But over a period of four or five years, the figure slowly, imperceptibly, unbeknown to Laxman himself, evolved and morphed into the present avuncular image who could be from any state and anybody's uncle or retired schoolteacher or government servant. And he stayed that way. Over fifty years, he never aged!

Laxman and his wife and also his daughter-in-law and son became family friends. Till his health stood him in good stead, Laxman and his wife took a short vacation and visited us every year and spent a few days on our farm in Hassan district and just relaxed, travelling to Coorg and other towns close by. He loved the rural towns and villages of old Mysore state and especially Hassan, where he grew up. Kamala was devoted to him and took care of him, aware that her ward was no ordinary human being.

I was fortunate to know him. Laxman was, I think, an agnostic. So am I. But when I see his artistic creativity and his prodigious output over six decades, I begin to wonder and conclude it must be God who worked through him.

*The Economic Times*, February 2015

# Jasraj, Who Could Sing 'Om Allah Om' on Ramanavami

About two months ago, quite out of the blue, I received a call from Pandit Jasraj. He had stayed with us on many occasions when he visited Bangalore on his concert tours. We didn't converse or call each other when he was travelling around India or overseas, but when he visited Bangalore, he usually chose to stay in our house. And when at times he stayed elsewhere, he would always call me and invite me to his performances, which I never missed. I was happy and surprised by his sudden call and asked him the reason for it. I imagined he might be planning to visit my city after a long gap. He said he was calling from the United States and he had been dividing his time between India and America over the last many years. He had numerous students there, was associated with a number of universities and was presently unable to come to India because of the COVID-19 situation. I wondered still as to the purpose of his call. He simply said he wanted to speak to a few friends with whom he shared good warm memories. He recalled his days in Bangalore at our home and asked about my wife. We chatted on, and I told him I looked forward to his visiting again.

The call by Panditji evoked a strange feeling in me. It warmed my heart and brought both a smile and tears. I mentioned to my wife that it seemed like it was a thanksgiving. I had a vague sense that Jasraj knew his time on the planet was drawing to a close.

The memories of those short stays at our home are still vivid. His silvery hair streaming behind, a glowing face, gentle eyes, a beatific and disarming smile, his soft-spoken winning ways and impeccable attire of spotless white dhotis with vibrant borders, worn in the traditional style and matched perfectly with colourful kurtas, are all still etched in my mind. There was a radiant aura around him. That imagery of an arresting and attractive persona was entwined with his melodic voice that penetrated your soul.

When he was with us, he was mostly indoors in his room. And the hum of his ragas, swaras and aalaps wafted across and filled the house. At times, there would be the strum of the tamboora or notes of the harmonium, too, when his accompanying artists came to visit him before the concert. To me, those melodies and strains are as precious as his grand concerts.

Often, there were streams of admirers who would walk in unannounced. It was a source of annoyance, but when we could snatch an hour alone with him, I would draw him into conversations about other music legends, both Hindustani and Carnatic singers. Once, he narrated an interesting experience that occurred during a concert festival in Kolkata many decades ago. He was a young artist at the time, and there was the much older but legendary Semmangudi Srinivas Iyer. They had both performed on the concert stage, but the highlight was Bade Ghulam Ali Khan, who had mesmerized the audience. When they were all together after their performances, Ustad Bade Ghulam Ali Khan complimented Jasraj, but he had special praise for Semmangudi. Bade Ghulam Saab apparently said to Semmangudi, 'You have great music in you. Your whole being embodies music and distinctions between Hindustani and Carnatic music vanished when I listened to you.' Artists have their own rivalries, but Jasraj had a generosity of spirit and genuine admiration for other great contemporary musicians such as Bhimsen Joshi.

Many of the legendary Hindustani singers and instrumentalists – Ustad Bade Ghulam Ali Khan, Abdul Karim Khan, Begum Akhtar, the Dagar Brothers, Vilayat Khan and Bismillah Khan, to name a few – practised Islam. But they sang and played instruments in praise of Hindu deities. Bade Ghulam Ali Khan's bhajan '*Hari Om Tat Sat*' is something that could figuratively transport one to heaven. So it was with Nadaswaram Samrat Sheikh Chinna Maulana Sahib. Temple musicians such as Ustad Bismillah Khan and Jesudas, who sang in all major temple festivals, mesmerized their audiences.

I still remember the day Pandit Jasraj and I drove together from my home to the famed annual Ramanavami festival at Fort High School in Bangalore. He sang for nearly four hours. He was eighty at the time. The dais was alongside the deity of Rama. Towards the end of the performance, he sang '*Mero Allah Meherbaan*' and '*Om Allah Om*'. Immersed in that divine music, I was floating as if in a trance along with the rasikas. Then, I caught the words Allah and Hari in the same notes. My heart swelled, and tears welled up in my eyes. He fused Om and Allah and dissolved himself and every one of us into that supreme reality. He held the audience in thrall doing so, just as he captivated us in an equal spell singing '*Om Namo Bhagawate Vasudeva*', his signature bhajan.

In that instant, he transcended all religious barriers and carried everyone into a celestial bliss. That, to me, is his greatest gift and legacy to India and the rest of mankind, which is today in real danger, 'broken up into fragments by narrow domestic walls'.

Pandit Jasraj must be singing to the gods and smiling down from the heavens. His melody continues to ring in our hearts. As poet P.B. Shelley said, 'Music, when soft voices die, vibrates in the memory.'

*Deccan Herald*, August 2020

# Girish Karnad Was Both Solitary and Solidary

A couple of years ago, Girish Karnad walked up to my wife at a dinner and said, 'I've been telling Captain to give the film rights to his book *Simply Fly* as it captures a vast canvas of life, full of colour and adventure from village life to his agricultural exploits, army and the war, helicopters and aviation. It lends itself to vivid cinematic expression. Please urge him. I'm ready to don the robes and war paint even now and play his role, and am ready to direct it!'

What touched me was his sheer exuberance, even at his seventy-nine years.

Girish was many things to many people because he was a man of many parts and facets – playwright, writer, theatre actor, film actor in multiple languages, director, screenwriter, humanist, activist, folklorist, scholar, institution builder and so on. But I was drawn to his sincerity, stoic courage and dignity in matters of public interest and on civic issues, religion, culture, the arts and freedom of expression.

Above all, he was free of cant and humbug. He had no airs about himself, and all shades of affected piety and sanctimonious nationalism were anathema to him. He lived as he preached, a modern-day Socrates.

When you know someone who is famous and admire them from a distance for their stellar qualities, impressed through their writings and by what they stand for, made familiar through the press, television and other mediums, and finally meet them face to face and find them true to the image you have of them, it doesn't feel like you're meeting them the first time. That's how it was when I met Girish around fifteen years ago.

The Karnad I was seeing for the first time was the palimpsest of the Karnads I had read, seen on screen and visualized in my mind's eye. Hence, I can't recall the first time I met him. We were not intimate friends, but we often met at functions. He came home without ado for dinners or classical concerts I hosted occasionally. He loved a good drink and enjoyed his meals. He had an arresting presence, and people were easily drawn to him. Yet he was reticent and would leave quietly if the gathering prolonged.

A man of his talents and multiple creative pursuits had to guard his privacy. Time was his jealous mistress. But he did not live in an ivory tower, like many creative writers do. He didn't feel privileged. He spoke his mind fearlessly, without raising his voice or haranguing others, free of any self-righteous pomposity, on issues that impinged on our civil liberties and the public good.

He participated in protests to make his views known but did not hanker after publicity, nor was he given to vulgar rhetoric. He maintained that delicate balance of being able to create, which demanded solitude, but was also immersed in contemporary issues; he was, as was said of Albert Camus, at once solitary and solidary. Not one without the other. His life affirmed that his art was meaningless and unworthy without solidarity.

Girish drew his sustenance from his rural town in Sirsi, deep in the Western Ghats, where he spent his childhood, and from Dharwad, the crucible of culture. The fount of his muse was Hindustani music and Kannada literature, Hindu mythology, folklore, folk dance and drama. He was as much in love with Marathi theatre as Kannada.

He was the last of the great literary figures and writers in Kannada, along with U.R. Ananthamurthy, who were scholars in English literature, and many of whom taught English in universities but wrote in Kannada, like T.N. Srikantaiah, B.M. Srikantaiah, A.N. Murthy Rao, K.V. Puttappa and D.R. Bendre. Girish was an Oxford and Rhodes scholar but returned to write in Kannada. He was a true 'native and to the manor born'. Like many bilingual and multilingual giants of that era, Karnad straddled the local, the regional, the national and the universal at the same time.

As Ramachandra Guha said, 'There is no one alive in India who so well understood and embodied the richness and the diversity of Indian culture in his life and in his work and in his writings than Karnad.' And in Karnad's own famous words, in his inimitable Kannada, 'You must be rooted deeply in land to be able to spread your wings in the sky.'

So, it was ironic he was dubbed an 'Urban Naxal' because none was more rooted in the soil than Girish. He was pained, and probably bemused, at the charges by shallow social media groups. If anything, he was urbane, whether he spoke in his chaste Dharwad Kannada and quoted Bendre with ease, whom he held in high esteem, or in Konkani, his mother tongue, or he cited Marathi writers and playwrights, or spoke in English and quoted lines from Shakespeare or Eugene O'Neill with equal aplomb. He was gentle, cultured and suave, but never elitist in tone or condescending in manner.

On the urban Naxal tag, he said, 'Polarization efforts are part of democracy; we must face it. Because of social media's emergence, it becomes controversial or sensational. I don't want to control it. That's how democracy works.' Even under attack and after receiving death threats, he swore by free speech. That was the true measure of the man; he had no rancour or bitterness.

Karnad embraced and celebrated life because there was no resentment. He had magnanimity and a generosity of spirit to admire what was good in people and among his fellow artists. He had reverence for writers and poets who celebrated the beauty of this world and the grandeur of the human spirit. But he did not hero worship.

A couple of years ago, when he criticized Tagore's plays, there was an uproar. It was sacrilege. Even I was upset. The media screamed, 'Karnad calls Tagore a second-rate poet.' When I heard Karnad himself in an interview, he said, 'I was speaking to the students of Premji University on the critical evaluation of Tagore's plays, in a particular context. I rate Tagore's poetry very highly. His *Gitanjali* is an extraordinary poem. He's a great thinker and humanist. I admire his views on nationalism. But I think his plays are second rate.'

He went on to add, 'There is no need to blindly hero-worship anyone. An artist's work should be critically seen.' A single line was taken out of context, and he was vilified. Karnad faced both criticism and praise with poise and restrained dignity.

He did not worship any icons, nor did he vilify anyone. He was totally apolitical, but he fiercely opposed all political parties with equal force if they trampled on human dignity and the universal brotherhood that poets and writers like Bendre, Kuvempu and Shivram Karanth, the Jnanpith awardees who preceded him, celebrated in their works. He sought no honours or publicity for himself either in life or death. He died as he lived, with simplicity and grace.

'Thus unlamented let me die;
Steal from the world, and not a stone
Tell where I lie.'

*The Wire*, Jun 2019

# Vajpayee, a Man for All Seasons: Fond Memories

I met Vajpayee on a couple of occasions, the first through luck and providence and the second by design. I had become the president of the BJP of Hassan by fortuitous circumstance. I had taken premature retirement from the army and had returned home to take up farming. I had made a name for myself in organic sericulture – mulberry farming and silkworm rearing. The BJP, which was in its infancy then in the country and non-existent in Karnataka, had approached me to join the party and lead it in Hassan as the president. The party was on a drive across the country to recruit laterally to its cadre retired army officers, civil servants and professionals like doctors and lawyers. The Congress ruled the roost, and the main opposition was from Devegowda's Janata's party, later Janata Dal, and he reigned over Hassan. No one wanted the post I was offered! It was the most un-coveted post. The mantle easily fell on me. I accepted the position with trepidation. The task was daunting. I was a total greenhorn in politics. This was in 1987/88.

Then one day, I received a call from the state BJP headquarters. Mr Atal Bihari Vajpayee was touring Karnataka and would be visiting Hassan. As the president, I was called upon to organize the reception and make all necessary arrangements for the visit and his address to the public in the district headquarters. There were huge expectations to make it a success.

It involved getting the grounds and administrative and police clearances for the venue, spreading the message across the district and mobilizing large crowds. All this meant one thing – big funds. Mobilizing the crowds was a Herculean task. Political parties typically hire lorries and tractors and ferry villagers and dole out a few hundred rupees with lunch to bring them to the venue. It is a kind of tamasha and picnic for the villagers. And it is usually a great success but gives no peep into the inscrutable minds of the people. I was reluctant to do this. The BJP coffers were empty, and I was myself living hand to mouth. I was nervous.

I chose the most effective way. I sent about twenty party workers to paint the message on all walls in as many villages and the taluq headquarters and distribute pamphlets announcing Vajpayee's visit. With a couple of hired autorickshaws adorned with banners on either side, we broadcast the message through loudspeakers. With volunteers in tow, we set about raising funds from the public. We then realized they offered sympathy but not donations. I realized, to my dismay, that no one wished to bet on a losing horse. However, a few prominent businessmen and small traders discreetly loosened their purse. I had to make do with what we had raised, which was meagre. And I just prayed for success, relying on Vajpayee's charisma. But knowing that this was a rural constituency deep in the south, unlike the Hindi heartland, I was filled with apprehensions.

In those days, the BJP office bearers came by bus or cars offered by friends and stayed and dined in various party workers' homes while on tour. The five-star hotel culture was not there. So that burden was absent. I took on the responsibility of hosting a dinner for Vajpayee along with those who accompanied him in my house after the speech. There would be about eight to ten guests. He was accommodated in the circuit house for the night.

A year ago, Rajiv Gandhi had come. I remember my mother going with her friends for the speech. He was young, handsome and had undeniable charisma with the Nehru lineage. He attracted massive crowds wherever he went. That played on my mind, and I waited with bated breath for Vajpayee's visit with nervous foreboding.

The day arrived. I received him in the guest house and was bowled over with his easy and charming manners and self-assurance without a trace of arrogance. Then I went and waited at the venue of his public address. The ground began to fill up. And by the time he arrived, it was filled to the point of overflowing. I was relieved and elated. His reputation as a great orator had preceded him, and his charisma had undeniably worked and saved the day. The weather held up, and it had nothing whatever to do with my organizational capabilities. Mr Vajpayee was impeccably and very elegantly dressed in his starched classic white dhoti tied in classic style, and khadi vest with a simple cotton stole. He spoke in chaste Hindi, but his Hindi was laden with Sanskrit words and most Kannadigas understood it with ease. He was mesmerizing, and the crowd was spellbound.

My wife had cooked a simple vegetarian old Mysore meal with a variety of dishes and a payasam of gusguse – poppy seeds. There was a light banter over dinner. Vajpayee put everyone at ease with his easy manners and wit. There was a debate in those days for allowing more liberal licensing for television channels, and the government of the day, stuck in the rut of the past, was reluctant to let go of the monopoly of Doordarshan, blind to the invasion of television in the West and the new Asian economies. I opened a debate. I asked Mr Vajpayee why he could not announce that when the BJP came to power, he would free the skies for the television and let a thousand TV and radio channels bloom. It would strengthen democracy, prevent a repeat of the Emergency that he had himself witnessed when he was jailed and knit the country together and provide thousands of jobs. He was taken aback. I was still young, brash and pompous and eagerly got into debates. Vajpayee shot back, 'Young man, do you know the consequences of privatizing television and radio? You know what will happen if it falls into the hands of terrorists?' Not one to give up, I retorted, 'Sir, it's easier to take over one government channel but not a thousand private ones.' We got into a vigorous exchange. Some of the senior worthies seemed worried and looked furtively at me and signalled to withdraw. Others tucked at the sleeves of my kurta. They were petrified that things may get out of hand and Vajpayee may get offended. When my wife went to serve the payasam, he looked quizzically at her. My wife deftly changed the subject and said it was made of poppy seeds and would give a sound sleep after a tiring day. It was a favourite Iyengar dessert. Vajpayee laughed heartily. He enjoyed the dessert. He loved good food and lively conversations. Dinner finished, we retired into the drawing room. Then I went up to him and said, 'Sorry, sir, if I was a bit aggressive and persisted with a contrarian view.' He thrust his hand out and mimicked a boxer as though to punch me and said, 'Captain, I like repartees, and I don't easily give up either!' And we all had a good laugh.

A few years later, I gave up politics and plunged into aviation and started a helicopter charter company. And almost a decade-and-half later after my meeting with Vajpayee in Hassan, when the wheels of political fortunes had turned in favour of the BJP and Vajpayee became the Prime Minister for the third time, I went to meet him. I had then embarked on my new venture to start the low-cost airline Air Deccan. My venture was bogged down in the morass of bureaucratic red tape, as was normal. I sought a meeting with him, wondering if he would still recall my brief meeting at Hassan. His eyes lit up with recognition when he saw me, and he enquired how I was. Then he said that he had flown often in Air Deccan helicopters before he became Prime Minister. I told him that I had left politics and embarked on aviation after my Hassan days as I felt I didn't possess the skills for that vocation. He said, 'Achha hua (Good thing),' with a glint and smile in his eyes. I was not sure if he meant it was good for politics or for me that l left politics. He had mischievous wit. I went on to explain that I had applied to the government to start a low-cost airline to make common people fly. And it was going nowhere. He understood instantly the purpose of my visit, being the reformer at heart that he was. He said, 'Nishchint raho. Aapke sapne udenge (Be free of worry and your dream will take wings).' I stood up, bowed to him, shook hands and left.

Air Deccan took to the skies within six months. Vajpayee was a genial man with a generous heart, good humour, free of cant and hypocrisy, loving, decent and humane and a great orator and poet with the common touch and common foibles. Rare in politics. That is why he was an adored leader. May he smile from the heavens.

*The Times of India*, August 2018

# A COVID-19 Death: When It Strikes Closer Home

'Wife died today.' The terse message was from my close cousin. After struggling on ventilator support for nearly a month in a Bangalore hospital, the coronavirus had got the better of her. It was devastating news.

The novel coronavirus. First, it was a mysterious disease. In distant lands. Eerie feelings of unease then crept in, reminding one of SARS and H1N1, the earlier viruses which came out of the blue, with visitations of death. The first coronavirus deaths were reported in China, and then in Italy and Spain, where the disease raged suddenly like a forest fire. And like a forest fire, it leapt over distances – only this time across vast spaces and oceans – and started devouring America. And then, it engulfed and ravaged India. Like a ghost, it stalked. It was nowhere but everywhere.

The daily infections and hospital admissions transcribed this macabre illness and its deaths onto news tickers on television and converted them into mere numbers and figures. Then statisticians morphed them into graphs for analysts. It was all dry and bald statistics – of deaths of nameless, faceless thousands. And stories in the papers and media and occasional anecdotes of people from our country who may have got infected with this illness or stranded on foreign shores were carried and conveyed to us through our social media groups. Then you saw here and there, around the world, news of celebrities getting infected with and succumbing to the virus.

For us, they were all television deaths. Even when the nation hunkered down in a forced lockdown and millions of migrants were on an exodus, dying of hunger, suffering from thirst and exhaustion on their long march, and many were mowed down by trucks and trains as they trudged home with their belongings and infants in their arms, the virus was still a faraway thing – an imagined disease. It was wished away by gloating, complacent politicians, sadhus and saints and charlatans with chants and gongs. Quacks and godmen dispensed native voodoo medicines made of bones and antlers, of dung and cow urine, and promoted pranic healing through yoga as a cure-all.

In a curious twist, when a godman, politician or celebrity coughed and went breathless, and their body temperatures soared, they rushed to modern hospitals in search of the best available allopathic care. And some did not make it. All these stories were still something you watched on raucous television shows, anchored by gladiators on steroids. You would watch them as you would a Bollywood masala movie.

But when the news hits you, when it shatters you like a stone flung at your living room glass window, that one of your close friends, a relative or an office colleague has been rushed to the hospital and put on a ventilator, and when you learn that their grief-stricken family can't visit them in the hospital and you can't even go and offer sympathies because the virus is hovering about – it is invisible but menacing, like the ghost of Banquo in Macbeth, haunting men who have a foreboding that this is retribution for all the sins committed by man not only against his fellow beings but against the planet – then a strange fear grips you. You feel impotent against the microcosm. And when the news arrives that the patient, whom you knew so well, whom you had met only recently, has passed away and that the doctors, overwhelmed by the mysterious disease, couldn't save your dear ones, then the reality hits you like a grenade exploding next to you. It is not a statistic anymore. It's not a conspiracy of the left-wing politicians out to destabilize the government. It's not an American right-wing delusion of a Chinese virus that escaped or was released wilfully from a Chinese lab. It's not a virus weaponized by Muslims to kill Hindus by infiltrating Hindu society as the 'IT cell' of some political party would want us to believe. It is, as all the reputed doctors and epidemiologists have said, a virus that is most virulent and lethal. It is a bizarre, deviant new virus about which little is known and which is taking scientists by surprise with its inscrutable behaviour, wreaking havoc, impacting the lives and livelihoods of every living being. Chest-beating and bravado, instead of respect for science, is the courage of ignorance that can be fatal to king and commoner.

The death of a close relative, a friend or a colleague by this virus is no longer mere data but is now very personal and touching. It is a double tragedy with the coronavirus – most COVID-19 patients not only suffer but also suffer and die alone. And this is unbearably tragic because their loved ones can't be near them when they take their last breath. They can't even see the body or cremate it with time-honoured rituals. What terrible loneliness for the dying! What horrors for those who wait helplessly with unspeakable anxiety!

Yet, despite such overwhelming odds stacked against us, pessimism, a dispirited outlook of futility, cannot be a choice. It is slow suicide. Science, and scientific temperament that is true to its core principles of tireless and honest pursuit of knowledge without cant, has solved and will continue to solve the problems of the human race if humans stop seeing themselves as a race superior, distinct and apart from Nature and the universe. And to even think that one religion, race or caste is superior to others is grossly vile and profane. It can only lead to disintegration. This harks back to the core of Indian philosophy – *tat tvam asi* (thou art that). All life, all matter, all beings are One. This must unite us to fight the virus.

Such an outlook of solidarity will awaken infinite hope. But that optimism has to be grounded in faith in science, and not jingoism. Nor is such optimism an option. As Karl Popper said, ‘Optimism is a duty today.’

*Deccan Herald*, October 2020

# Our Folk Tradition Has a Lesson for Those Communalising Classical Music

Recently, I chanced upon a television debate titled 'Is Carnatic music getting communalized?' As is normal nowadays, when topics are sensitive, the debate rages and goes into high decibels, with everyone screaming over each other, the anchor feebly attempting to control the talking heads but soon drowning in the cacophony. On the show, I recognized well-known and reputed Carnatic classical singer and Magsaysay Award winner T.M. Krishna, who has been at the forefront of taking classical music to tribal and transgender communities and other marginalized sections of society. He holds concerts in their hamlets, involving the youth, and performs along with them in their communities, mingling in their midst and recognizing their music as not being inferior to classical forms of music but just different and often more vibrant and soulful. He has been on a musical journey that breaks social and caste barriers, often courting controversy along the way.

Through the heated debate, I could get the drift and gist of the charges being traded. Krishna was under siege from Hindu religious right-wing groups for defending a few of his musician colleagues for singing Carnatic music at Christian institutions. According to them, it was disrespectful to Hinduism; it was blasphemy. Krishna, called by many as the *enfant terrible* of Carnatic classical music and who revelled in that role, declared that music is universal and that it was being communalized by people who were bigoted, narrow-minded and ignorant. He quoted Muslim Sufi saint singers who composed songs on Krishna and Rama and cited the most revered Carnatic classical music composer Muthuswamy Dikshitar (referred to as one of the musical trinity, the other two being Tyagaraja and Shyama Shastri) who wrote Sanskrit lyrics to Western tunes, revealing his sparkling creativity and inclusiveness of the Indian spirit.

Soon after the debate, I received multiple messages expressing outrage at these artists 'selling their souls' to Christian missionaries. Appeals and petitions were circulated across social media, attacking some very well-known and popular Carnatic classical singers like Nityashree Mahadevan, O.S. Arun and Unnikrishnan accusing them of substituting, for example, the saint composer Tyagaraja's name in the krithi or lyric with Prabho or Yesu (Jesus) in his compositions. There were appeals exhorting people – 'Let us join hands in saving our religion.' There were others who made charges that appeared a bit bizarre, calling this a vandalization of music and urging people not to allow Christianization and cultural appropriation of Carnatic music on the suspicion that the churches and missionaries would use this to convert Hindus to Christianity.

It was reported that apart from verbal abuses, physical threats began to be issued to the artists on social media. That is when Krishna stood up for his colleagues, though they themselves retreated and were not fighting back. Many singers issued apologies and cancelled their engagements, unwilling to get into controversies with aggressive self-styled groups representing Hindu outfits.

O.S. Arun is a prominent Carnatic classical artist who is known more for singing devotional Carnatic songs of saints from the south and who has also popularized Marathi abhangs and bhajans of Meera and Kabir among the southern audience. Over the telephone, a member of a right wing group asked him: 'Why are you singing for Christians, being a Hindu?' Arun responded that the Hindu dharma teaches its worshippers to respect all religions. He added that one of his shows was cancelled because of certain threats, which he did not want to disclose further.

A Twitter war broke out and continues between Krishna, who took up the cause of his fellow musicians, and the right-wing groups and their supporters. There are also a large number of supporters praising and admiring Krishna for his stand, which is evident in the comments he received on his Twitter post.

Many of the legendary Hindustani singers and instrumentalists – Ustad Bade Ghulam Ali Khan, Abdul Karim Khan, Begum Akhtar, Dagar Brothers, Vilayat Khan and Bismillah Khan, to name a few – practiced Islam. But they sang and played instruments that were in praise of Hindu deities. Ustad Bade Ghulam Ali Khan's bhajan '*Hari Om Tat Sat*' has the potential to figuratively transport the listener to heaven. So with Nadaswaram Samrat Sheikh Chinna Maulana Sahib. Temple musicians such as Ustad Bismillah Khan and Jesudas sang in all major temple festivals, mesmerizing their audience. Who has not been moved by Pandit Jasraj singing a bhajan on Allah, '*Mero Allah Meherbaan*' or '*Om Allah Om*', where he fuses Om and Allah and dissolves both into that supreme reality? I heard him sing this in Bangalore at the Ramanavami festival at the Fort High School a few years ago. He held the audience in thrall just as he holds one in an equal spell while singing '*Om Namo Bhagawate Vasudeva*'. These artists have transcended all religious barriers through their music. Music, like sports, is a great unifier.

And who can ever forget Gandhi's immortal bhajan '*Raghupati Raghava Raja Ram, Iswara Allah Tero Naam*'? It was sung and popularized by Pandit Vishnu Digambar Paluskar, a Hindustani singer and pioneer who shaped Hindustani music, taking it to the masses.

In India, Sufism and Sufi music, with its mysticism inspired by its poets and saints, converged with the Bhakti movement and its devotional music. Both were neutral to conventional religion without its strict tenets and codes. They were mystical in nature but intrinsically reformist and preached simplicity, love, harmony, peace and devotion to God expressed through longing for oneness with the divine, in the broadest sense of those words. It is widely held that they influenced not only each other but also Sikhism, Jainism and Buddhism. All classical singers of yesterday and today from both schools sing songs of both the Sufi and the Bhakti poet-saints. Kabir is a prime example of the quintessential saint transcending narrow religious divides and is equally revered by Muslims, Hindus and Sikhs and appropriated by all three with pride. Who has not sung Kabir's bhajans?

Rabindranath Tagore was greatly influenced and inspired by the Bauls and also translated some of their songs. A group of wandering mystic minstrels, a sect who mainly compose of Vaishnava Hindus and Sufi Muslims, the Bauls hail from both Bangladesh and West Bengal. Many of our medieval devotional poems, including folk songs from every part of India, are steeped in messages of non-sectarian devotion through the love of the divine and worship of nature. They all have one common thread of belief: search for God not through temples or mosques or churches, as God is within yourself. You yourself have to seek him individually. Here is a Baul song, in Tagore's translation, which best expresses it:

> The man of my heart dwells inside me. Everywhere I behold,
> it's Him! In my every sight, in the sparkle of light
> Oh I can never lose Him —
> Here, there and everywhere,
> Wherever I turn, right in front is He!

We all need a good dose of Baul folk poetry and its wisdom to save ourselves from being 'broken up into fragments by narrow domestic walls'.

*The Wire*, August 2018

# Beyond Good and Evil

The horrifying crimes in Kathua and Unnao remind one of the existential and perennial problem of evil in Dostoevsky's novel *The Brothers Karamazov*, in which Ivan Karamazov confronts his younger brother Alyosha, the young monk, and questions him on the justification of evil in this world, especially against children.

'A Bulgarian I met lately in Moscow,' Ivan continues, seeming not to hear his brother's words, 'told me about the crimes committed by Turks and Circassians in all parts of Bulgaria ... They burn villages, murder, outrage women and children, they nail their prisoners by the ears to the fences, leave them so till morning, and in the morning they hang them – all sorts of things you can't imagine. People talk sometimes of bestial cruelty, but that's a great injustice and insult to the beasts; a beast can never be so cruel as a man, so artistically cruel. The tiger only tears and gnaws, that's all he can do. He would never think of nailing people by the ears, even if he were able to do it. These Turks took a pleasure in torturing children, too; cutting the unborn child from the mother's womb, and tossing babies up in the air and catching them on the points of their bayonets before their mother's eyes. Doing it before the mother's eyes was what gave zest to the amusement. Here is another scene that I thought very interesting. Imagine a trembling mother with her baby in her arms, a circle of invading Turks around her. They've planned a diversion; they pet the baby, laugh to make it laugh. They succeed, the baby laughs. At that moment a Turk points a pistol four inches from the baby's face. The baby laughs with glee, holds out his little hand to the pistol, and he pulls the trigger in the baby's face and blows out its brains. Artistic, wasn't it? …'

The problem of evil in the world has agitated the minds of many great sages and philosophers since ages. How do you explain the existence of evil, where innocent people are tortured and children raped and murdered, not to mention the questions that arise when you look at pain and cruelty on animal life and devastation caused by natural calamities that maim and kill thousands of people, indiscriminately causing senseless misery? But the torture and killing of children just numbs you and is beyond the pale of all understanding.

Ivan continues, 'Listen! I took the case of children only to make my case clearer. I have narrowed my subject on purpose. Of the other tears of humanity with which the earth is soaked from its crust to its centre, I will say nothing. If all must suffer to pay for the eternal harmony, what have children to do with it, tell me, please? It's beyond all comprehension why they should suffer, and why they should pay for the harmony … I renounce the higher harmony altogether. It's not worth the tears of that one tortured child … And if the sufferings of children go to swell the sum of sufferings which was necessary to pay for truth, then I protest that the truth is not worth such a price.'

Ivan goes on animatedly and asks Alyosha how he can explain such cruelty and pain. 'Is there a God? Even if there's one I do not accept him. I reject him on the plane of justice.'

If there's an all-powerful, beneficent God, how do you explain evil and the cruel crimes that the world has witnessed these thousands of years – wars, pogroms, hunger, pestilence, floods, torture, cruelty and killings of millions over centuries that we continue to see every day? God, as is commonly believed and conceptualized, is all beneficent, all good, omnipotent, omniscient and omnipresent, and such a God cannot be reconciled with a world that has so much evil, pain and suffering. It is a 'logical impossibility'.

As Epicurus, the Greek philosopher, expounded, famously called The Epicurean Trilemma:

> Is God willing to prevent evil, but not able? Then he is not omnipotent.
> Is he able, but not willing? Then he is malevolent.
> Is he both able and willing? Then whence cometh evil?
> Is he neither able nor willing? Then why call him God?

## A futile question

All philosophers and even mystics stumble at this point. When asked on many occasions about evil, Tagore said, 'Asking why there's evil in this world is like asking why there's creation! It is a futile question. You have to accept it simply as part of evolution toward perfection.'

Charles Darwin said, 'The sufferings of millions of the lower animals throughout almost endless time are apparently irreconcilable with the existence of a creator of unbounded goodness.'

History has shown that the world is not evolving towards perfection on the lines the believers of theistic religions have argued with implicit faith. Evil has not diminished over the years but has only increased and with more ingenuity, novelty and heartlessness in methods of torture and cruelty and in inflicting immeasurable pain, injustice and killings, aided by weapons, chemicals and modern technology. We have more blood and tears spilt as days go by towards eternity.

The Kathua rape of an eight-year-old girl, her gruesome torture and murder, the horrific rape of a seventeen-year-old girl in Unnao and the murder of her father by the alleged rapists and their cohorts have shaken the people across the country to their very core, not only because the heinous nature of the crimes is so hard to fathom and goes against innate human nature but also because of the apathy and depravity of those in power and their followers in the way they responded to the crime and the religious, communal and caste overtones that overshadowed the tragedies. These are blood-curdling and spine-chilling.

The images of the luminous face of the girl in Kathua and the grief and despair of her parents and siblings, the helpless cries of the minor girl in Unnao for justice not only against those who violated her but murdered her father and caused her and her mother unfathomable sorrow will haunt us for years to come.

## Widespread condemnation

Beyond the degrading politics on both sides of the divide, the people of India, cutting across all religious, caste and socio-economic divisions, rose in one voice and unequivocally condemned the rapes and killings, which is heartening. Justice in this world is all that we know and what everyone is demanding. There is no place either for justice and harmony in an after-life or justification of the horrendous crimes through theories of karma.

Justice in India today is so long in delivery; it is akin to the promised justice of many religions in heaven in another world that no one has certainty of, or the utopia promised in the future by communism, where all crimes and evils are justified today for a future classless and ideal society.

When there are crimes by demented and deranged people, they may at times be overlooked and treated as isolated cases of 'sick' individuals and can be considered extenuating. But what is deeply unsettling and terrifying is when crimes are perpetrated with brazen disregard to the rule of law on grounds of ideological, religious, communal or caste differences or when those crimes and acts of cruelty are carried out by those in power over the powerless, the weak and the defenceless with crass impunity. Nothing, absolutely nothing, can absolve anyone from crimes against them, especially crimes of rape and murder when the victims are children and minors.

In the end, beyond all analysis of good and evil, crimes like these are simply unacceptable. It is organic repulsion by human nature. As Ivan says to Alyosha, '… all I know is that there is suffering and that there are none guilty; … and I can't consent to live by it! I must have justice, or I will destroy myself. And not justice in some remote infinite time and space, but here on earth, and that I could see myself.'

CNBC TV18, April 2018

# Coronavirus Outbreak: Let's Learn from Socrates

A journalist called me a couple of days ago seeking an interview. The central question was: Will the aviation sector survive the coronavirus pandemic?

That made me reflect. Do I have the answer? Do I really know how the world would pan out three to six months hence?

After a couple of hours, I sent this reply: 'I've honest misgivings about my ability to offer any insight. I mean, predicting anything on this epidemic about which so little is known, and based on that half-baked knowledge offering cure or counsel about aviation, I will be no better than the quacks who are peddling cow urine as a cure for the coronavirus. I will be like the modern-day godmen who hop around in helicopters, surrounded by lovely women sashaying in silk, and dispensing instant "nirvana". One of them said drinking fiery hot rasam can kill the virus; another, that "You can test yourself if you have the coronavirus by doing pranayam after yoga and holding your breath for 30 seconds. If you can't, then you know you have the virus."

'I'm sorry you may think I've digressed from 'aviation', but how can aviation be looked at independently? If millions of labourers and small farmers, the very backbone of the economy, are deprived of their livelihoods and income, then can the automobile or the airline industry, on top of the pyramid, survive when the base collapses? Don't you think we should postpone this interview for a while till we can make some sense of all this? I hesitate to wear the mantle of an "oracle".'

After I had thus declined the invitation in a long-winded manner, my mind went back several years to my childhood. There was a prolonged drought once, and our village was under the grip of famine. Cattle were dying. Food had become scarce. The poor begged for jobs. And one day, I saw a procession of villagers with sounds of drums and cymbals and pipes and people dancing. As it came in front of my house, I saw my mother carry a copper pitcher of water to the centre of the dancing throng. There, in the middle, was a strange sight. Instead of a deity, there were a few frogs tied to a plank, which was being carried by two bare-bodied youth. My mother poured the cold water on the frogs, who were wriggling under the hot sun, and performed 'aarti' on them. As she came back into the house, my father, an agnostic, muttered, 'Fools!' I watched in amazement and asked him what it meant. With a smile, he mocked, 'Just like those poor villagers; your mother also believes in the age-old superstition that if rains fail, you offer pooja and bathe the toads, then the heavens will send showers.'

We were a joint family in my early years. One day, I overheard that my granduncle's wife was his fourth wife. I was stunned. My father, trying to hide a smirk, said, 'She is actually the third wife. The first two wives died in quick succession, one after the other, soon after he married them. Then the number three, being an unlucky number, and to break the jinx of deaths, his third marriage was performed with a live banana tree, and after the symbolic ceremony, the tree was killed by cutting it in two. After that, he married his present wife.' Then he chuckled mischievously and continued, 'But the banana sacrifice may not prevent him from being widowed again. He ill-treats her all the time. God only knows when she may take her own life.'

Such were the superstitions of our ancestors, but when you see our modern-day gurus and political masters and their disciples preaching rubbish, you ask, will the new demon, the invisible virus, be killed by chants and cymbals or will the pathogen be stopped by virologists and vaccine-makers? Can the scourge be conquered by prophets or men of science? Will the 'guru' chant a 'mantra' when his tooth aches or go to the dentist? We all know the answer to that because truth will ultimately out. So, at the core, it is about stopping fooling oneself. Then, you will stop fooling the public.

Now, coming to our real crisis of life and death. There may be an answer, a glimmer of hope to conquer this crisis if we go back to what we learnt in our school days – to the historical figure, Socrates, considered the wisest man who ever lived. He admitted unhesitatingly, explicitly, that he did not know. And from that admission of ignorance, he gained indomitable courage and strength to question those who peddled falsehoods.

The physicist and Nobel laureate Richard Feynman said, 'The scientist has a lot of experience with ignorance and doubt and uncertainty, and this experience is of very great importance … Our freedom to doubt was born out of a struggle against authority in the early days of science. It was a very deep and strong struggle: "permit us to question, to doubt, to not be sure …" This is not a new idea; this is the idea of the age of reason. This is the philosophy that guided the men who made the democracy that we live under. The idea that no one really knew how to run a government led to the idea that we should arrange a system by which new ideas could be developed, tried out, and tossed out if necessary … doubt and discussion were essential to progress into the unknown. If we want to solve a problem that we have never solved before, we must leave the door to the unknown ajar …'

This crisis is so unprecedented that there are no lessons from history on how to deal with it. It has to be fought through collaboration – of minds and efforts – and not by noble intentions or intuitions alone. So, if our political leaders simply admit that they do not know and, with humility and without losing any more time, bring together the best brains of India from across the world – scientists, epidemiologists, doctors, economists, social scientists, etc. – to find the best way forward, an answer will emerge how best to fight this unknown terror and save both lives and livelihoods. As the *Rigveda* says, 'Let noble thoughts come to us from every side.'

*Deccan Herald*, April 2020

# Did God Just Roll the Dice? Or Did Nature, Like a Mathematical Equation, Simply Balance Itself?

When man kills a fellow being, he does so for many reasons. It could be because he is overcome by hatred or because he wants revenge, or maybe he kills for greed. Sometimes he does it in a fit of passion. And when he belongs to a religious order or fringe group, he is so radicalized by a political or revolutionary ideology that he slaughters others swayed by bigotry. Then there are the wars fought over misplaced nationalism, unleashed by leaders intoxicated with power, which take thousands of innocent lives.

In contrast, animals kill for hunger. But when God kills – through pandemics, pestilence, earthquakes and floods – you wonder, can God be so evil? Is it a cruel sport? Or is there a method to his mad fury?

No religious leader or mystic has been able to satisfactorily explain the problem of evil – the death of countless innocents at the hands of an omnipotent, all-merciful god. When Tagore was asked why there was evil, he said it was the same as asking why there was good. Now, we are visited by the coronavirus. To what purpose and design? Is nature acting in accordance with predetermined laws of the universe? Was Einstein wrong when he said, 'God does not play dice with the universe?'

The many misfortunes that befall mankind are explained away variously. Many believe the Old Testament that says the sins of the fathers are visited upon the children. A Hindu might explain that the tragedy is your karma for past misdeeds. A philosopher may blame it on the hubris of man. A scientist might say that the 'new man', intoxicated with pride and greed, cocksure about his knowledge and power, is destroying the planet. And that the pandemic is a punishment by nature for upsetting natural harmony.

## Fine balance

When the forests, soil, rivers, oceans, ice caps and atmosphere as well as the flora and fauna on the earth are depleted and, in many cases, wiped out, there is an impact on human beings, who play a minuscule part in the larger ecological web but have a symbiotic relationship with it. When this fine ecological balance is disturbed, humans cannot stay untouched. There is cause and effect. And a price is always paid.

Bertrand Russell, in his celebrated essay 'Men Versus Insects', written eighty-seven years ago, prophetically wrote that the threat to the human race might be as much from insects and micro-organisms as from wars. '… we no longer have occasion, like the cavemen, to fear lions and tigers, mammoths and wild boars. Except against each other, we feel ourselves safe … safe, except from the little creatures – the insects and the micro-organisms. Insects have an initial advantage in their numbers. A small wood may easily contain as many ants as there are human beings in the whole world. They have another advantage in the fact that they eat our food before it is ripe for us. If human beings, in their rage against each other, invoke the aid of insects and micro-organisms, as they certainly will do if there is another big war, it is by no means unlikely that the insects will remain the sole ultimate victors. Perhaps, from a cosmic point of view, this is not to be regretted; but as a human being I cannot help heaving a sigh over my own species.' But Russell could not imagine that man would race towards self-annihilation by means other than war. He did not foresee that man, blinded by avarice and pride, would simply axe off the base of the ecological tree atop which he was perched.

In nature, no excess goes unpunished; there's retribution for every trespass. And nature always has ways of compensation. I remember as a child going along with my father, a teacher in the local village school, to our rice fields in the mornings during planting season in the monsoons. He would point to the Dalits, men and women covered with conical raincoats made of straw and reeds, planting the saplings and singing in the rain. My father would show me the two sacks they carried under each arm. Into one, they stuffed the wild greens and spinach they plucked as they worked, and into the other, they tossed the crabs that scurried in the shallow waters. My father used to say that God was compensating the poor with free food. That message stayed with me – that there was an underlying law of compensation enacted one way or another in this very life. Nature compensates in strange ways when someone is robbed or defrauded. It unfailingly acts as a leveller.

## Life and maths

Speaking of this self-correcting and compensating nature of the universe, Ralph Waldo Emerson said, 'If the government is cruel, the governor's life is not safe. If you tax too high, the revenue will yield nothing. If you make the criminal code sanguinary, juries will not convict. If the law is too mild, private vengeance comes in. Justice is not postponed. A perfect equity adjusts its balance in all parts of life. The dice of 'god' are always loaded.'

The world is a bit like a mathematical equation – turn it how you will; it will balance itself. Cause and effect, means and ends, seed and fruit cannot be separated. For the effect already blooms in the cause, the end pre-exists in the means, the fruit in the seed.

There used to be a belief that there was a scientific, provable mathematical law of the universe, determined by these immutable laws. But the quantum mechanics of Heisenberg, Schrödinger and Dirac proved that the motion of atoms and electrons was indeterminate and random, that the ways of the universe were unpredictable. Stephen Hawking said, 'Thus it seems that even 'god' is bound by the Uncertainty Principle, and cannot know both the position and the speed of a particle. So god does play dice with the universe ... He still has a few tricks up his sleeve.'

And so you ask in amazement, is this pandemic a prank by god? Or is it nature's retribution for our pettiness, hatred, violence, bigotry, greed, arrogance and excess? Or is it just a random roll of the dice?

*The Hindu*, April 2020

# Every Man Is a Part of the Main

In the Kannada novel *Samskara: A Rite for a Dead Man* by Jnanpith awardee U.R. Ananthamurthy, the upper caste Brahmins in a village deep in rural north Karnataka, who are caught in the grip of an epidemic, face existential dilemmas. Their deeply held religious beliefs and rituals are being tested. The chief priest of the village, Praneshacharya, a devout, austere Brahmin, has to provide the answers. His neighbour, Naranappa, an irreverent, rebellious Brahmin who has a hedonistic lifestyle and who mocks the Brahmins and their rituals and their superstitions, suddenly takes ill and dies.

## Story of contrasts

There is no one to bury Naranappa even as his body begins to decompose inside his house in the 'Agrahara', the Brahmin quarters, because the Brahmins fear they may invite the wrath of the gods and worry about being excommunicated by the head priest of the mutt for cremating a renegade and heretic. They appeal to Praneshacharya to consult the scriptures and find an answer to the problem. Praneshacharya immerses himself in holy texts and prayers, but no revelations come to him.

As the days roll by, rats in their thousands die and lie strewn all over the streets, while vultures begin hovering over Naranappa's house. More people start dying in the village, and the epidemic kills without discrimination. The village is under the deadly scourge of the plague. The Brahmins are hungry and are not allowed to eat until the cremation is completed. Chandri, Naranappa's companion, is distraught as Dalits cannot enter the Agrahara and refuse to come to her aid. She offers all her jewellery to Praneshacharya and urges him to give it to the Brahmins to bury Naranappa. The Brahmins have by now eaten stealthily. A few relatives of Naranappa lay claim to the jewellery and lobby with Praneshacharya; if they get the jewellery, they will cremate Naranappa. They argue that there may be some provisions in the holy books whereby Naranappa can be cremated under the circumstances they find themselves in.

The scholarly Praneshacharya, who is steeped in iron-clad traditions, is aghast by the unscrupulous behaviour and the greed and does not give his consent until he finds an answer in the holy books. Unable to find any guidance, he heads to a temple beyond the village across the woods and seeks refuge in prayers in the temple. On his way back to the village, well past midnight, he meets Chandri in the forest, who stops him and falls at his feet. He is soon swept away by her irresistible attraction. When he wakes up at sunrise, he is overcome by shame and remorse, unable to face the Brahmins who are waiting for an answer. He leaves the village under the cover of darkness, devastated.

Chandri, who is desperate to get Naranappa buried at all costs before the body is devoured by rodents, gets a Muslim merchant, a friend, who commiserates with her helplessness, to cart away the rotting body with her help and cremate it.

This is a powerful story that shatters you and exposes the venality and hypocrisy and heartlessness of the upper castes and at the same time juxtaposes it and reveals the joyful, earthy humaneness and magnanimity of the peasants and the Dalits and the robust, healthy, cheerful outlook of a lone Muslim merchant of the town, who finds strength and common purpose in fraternity and solidarity, rising above petty differences.

## Many meanings

Then, there is another era and continent, a different context, in Albert Camus' *The Plague*. Here, in the city of Oran in Algeria, an epidemic of bubonic plague breaks out. As dead rats start piling on the streets and people start dying, the authorities, who are in denial and indifferent to the deaths, finally impose a quarantine. Overnight, the people of the city find themselves imprisoned. The total seclusion affects their daily lives and the impact on families suddenly separated from their loved ones throws the town into hysteria and panic. A priest uses the opportunity of the plague and, invoking his god, preaches refuge in religion to overcome the deadly attack to advance his own standing in the town.

*The Plague* can be read at many levels. On one level, it depicts the human condition when natural disasters sweep a city and affect everyone without discrimination and hold sway over the destiny of human beings caught in such a tragedy. It is also about sacrifice, love, friendship, generosity and connectedness while facing death collectively through stoic courage by confronting external forces beyond one's control through fraternity and solidarity. And the story also speaks of the pettiness and cowardice of those who flee from their responsibilities to the community. On another level, it is an allegorical depiction of the French Resistance against Nazi occupation during World War II. The plague is a metaphor for Hitler and the invading German Army.

On the other hand, when you are under siege (as happened to the Jews under Hitler and to France and other countries of Europe that were under occupation by the Nazis during World War II) or condemned to live under dictators who are an embodiment of evil (as in Stalinist Russia), when life and death are both uncertain or when you are caught in the inexorable vortex of events of history (such as the partition of India and Pakistan, or the Sikh massacres of Delhi in 1984, the Gujarat riots of 2002, the Syrian war or the recent riots in north-eastern Delhi), and when you have nowhere to run or hide, you realize you may be swept away in the tsunami of hate. You are fated to die, maybe perchance to live and your house, shop or factory may go up in flames depending on your caste, religion, belief and the colour of your skin. In times of riots and sectarian clashes that may suddenly flare up or that are stoked by vile politicians and community leaders, and if they rage across regions, and if you happen to be a Jew in a Muslim neighbourhood, or a Black or coloured person caught in a white supremacist area, or a Hindu in a Muslim-dominated mohalla, or a Muslim in a Hindu-majority district, or a Dalit in an upper caste locality or a Yazidi or a Christian in a territory invaded by the Islamic State, your destiny is not in your hands. It is determined by your race and religion and colour. It is decided by the vile things men do when their heart is ruled by hatred, bigotry, obscurantism, stupidity, fanaticism and a lust for power.

## Only destruction

When a pandemic, a tsunami, an earthquake or a flood ravages mankind, it devours everyone – the infants and the elderly, the men and the women, the sick and the healthy, all races of all religions and people irrespective of their ideological and political denominations. It is blind in its fury and swallows everything in its path, relentless and implacable as it marches on.

A communal or racial flare-up, though, may appear to the blinded zealot to be to their benefit or to their community's advantage; in the end, the blazing fire of hate will engulf everyone. It will spare no one from both sides of the conflict. It is more destructive than the natural disaster wrought by the gods and is sure to annihilate all.

There is only one way. We must all band together to fight evil. Whether the evil is a scourge of a pandemic such as the novel coronavirus outbreak or whether the evil deeds are perpetrated by a few who stoke the fire of hatred, in the end, let us not forget that it will devour us all.

As the poet John Donne poignantly said, 'No man is an island, entire of itself; every man is a piece of the continent, a part of the main, … Any man's death diminishes me, because I'm involved in mankind. And therefore never send to know for whom the bell tolls; it tolls for thee.'

*The Hindu*, March 2020

# The Return of the Native

When news broke that Parag Agrawal became CEO of Twitter, following in the footsteps of Sundar Pichai of Google and Satya Nadella of Microsoft and others, there was effusive praise about the rise of Indians in the United States. But the joy of their achievements is overshadowed by the loss for India. Is it the state of affairs of our country, our own failings, or is it simply their apathy or just the lure of lucre that draws them to foreign shores? It has been a steady loss of Indian talent over the last five decades. These were among our most gifted young men and women from our premier institutions who migrated after securing subsidized education, a fact that leaves a twinge of pain.

A thought crossed my mind about the many Indians who had gone abroad for higher studies to the West around a century ago, who gave up successful and lucrative careers, who did not yield to the temptation to stay but returned to India. And they did so during India's bleakest times and became a source of inspiration and a beacon of light to countless people who joined them to win our independence and to struggle to remove poverty, ignorance, social evils and injustice. They saw the same India as the others and sought to make it better rather than dismissing it as hopeless and making their lives elsewhere when they had the chance to do so.

These men and women are part of our recent history and lore, whose triumphs over trials and tribulations, indomitable courage and dedication and sacrifices to uplift our people are awe-inspiring.

Gandhi, who had a fairly prosperous legal practice in South Africa after becoming a barrister in England, returned to India. He is universally known, and his life is deified. The saga of Ambedkar is even more stirring and inspiring. A Dalit who grew up in extreme poverty, whose family suffered untouchability, went on to study in two of the most iconic institutions – Columbia University in the United States and the London School of Economics in the United Kingdom – earning from these institutions not one but two doctorate degrees in economics. He was also a barrister at law from Gray's Inn, a scholar in economics, law and political science and the architect of our Constitution. He dedicated his entire life to the upliftment of Dalits.

The sacrifices of Jawaharlal Nehru, born to a wealthy father, Motilal Nehru, and educated at Harrow and Cambridge, who too became a barrister after training in-law at the Inner Temple and who gave up everything and sailed to India to join the freedom movement, ignites your mind and heart. The tales of Bose, who returned from Cambridge, and his daring leadership in the Congress, and later that of Azad Hind Fauj, are electrifying. Sardar Patel saved up money to go to London, trained in law at the Middle Temple Inn and became a barrister after topping his class, but took a ship back to India to later join Gandhi's freedom struggle.

The lives of Aurobindo Ghosh, the revolutionary who returned from Cambridge and became a mystic, and Sarojini Naidu, the poet known as the Nightingale of India, alumni of King's College London and Cambridge, who came back and plunged into the freedom struggle, animate and swell your heart.

Shyama Prasad Mukherjee became a barrister after graduating from Lincoln's Inn but initially came back to join the Congress, later led the Hindu Mahasabha, distanced himself from it over the assassination of Gandhi, became a minister in Nehru's cabinet, quit and went on to found the Bharatiya Jan Sangh, the forerunner to the BJP.

Their stories and their struggles, the adventures of their minds, their reformist zeal and inextinguishable optimism and their love for the country invigorate and fascinate you. They returned to a country in its darkest period of oppression by the British, riven by factions and internal strife, a caste and communal cauldron, and to a people mired in poverty. They faced beatings and bullets and long prison sentences. And it is troubling that while those extraordinary individuals chose to return to repair our society's ills, those who are making a beeline to America and leaving the country are doing it because of our overwhelming problems – lack of opportunity, casteism and flawed reservations, social and communal strife, corruption and an ecosystem that does not reward merit.

Why have our young become anaesthetized to the ills of our society? Why are they turning their back on India and heading to the West? Why is a similar zeal and fervour missing today? Have globalization and technology desensitized and deadened our nobler feelings and sentiments? Is it a blind worship of the West and its opulence that has dulled our senses? Why are those who have settled abroad, despite their good jobs, more insecure today and increasingly jingoistic in advising their kin here to 'preserve our culture' and 'Hindu supremacy'? That is worrying and unworthy of our glorious civilization and heritage.

In the years before Independence and post-Independence, right up till 1974, when the US and western sanctions kicked in, the likes of Nehru and Indira Gandhi and Homi Bhabha and Vikram Sarabhai would recruit and send hundreds of freedom fighters, scientists and engineers, artists and academics, leaders and managers abroad and provide them with opportunities to come back and serve India.

Thus, Jayaprakash Narayan, initially fired up by the son-of-the-soil patriotism of Maulana Abul Kalam Azad, returned from the University of Wisconsin and joined the Indian National Congress on Jawaharlal Nehru's invitation and became a hero of the Quit India

Movement, later going on to oppose Indira Gandhi and Emergency, galvanizing the youth of the country and the opposition parties. Then there's Verghese Kurien, whom the Nehru government sent off to study nuclear engineering but who came back to be sent to Anand to build the Amul dairy movement. Hundreds, if not thousands, of nuclear and space scientists and engineers went abroad thus and came back to serve India's strategic programmes. Others built the civilian science institutions and workforce, and still others came back to teach at the IITs, Indian Institutes of Management (IIM), and All India Institutes of Medical Sciences (AIIMS).

Those who cross the oceans to discover and conquer new lands should be celebrated with generosity, whatever our reservations. But all those, from all religious denominations, who are keen to come back to their motherland must be embraced with open hearts and arms, invoking in them the spirit of our ancient verse from the Ramayana: 'Janani Janmabhumischa Swargadapi Gariyasi (Mother and motherland are superior to even heaven)'.

*Deccan Herald*, December 2021

# The Better Part of Valour

The tragic death of Chief of Defence Staff General Bipin Rawat reminded me of my days in the army and in civil aviation. When the Indian Air Force's (IAF) Tupolev-124 with Prime Minister Morarji Desai on board crashed near Jorhat, Assam, on 4 November 1977, all the five crew members died. Desai's entourage and an under-trainee flight engineer, who were not in the cockpit, survived. I remember Desai's words as quoted by the media after he walked out of the smouldering wreckage: 'I survived. My faith in God has been reinforced.' I was deputed to take a small contingent of my unit's soldiers to pay respects to Squadron Leader Mathew Cyriac, the co-pilot, whose funeral rites were held in Trivandrum, where I was posted. As I laid the wreath, I saw Cyriac's wife sobbing and their daughter playing with another child. I never forgot Desai's words. I couldn't help wondering whether God plays cruel games with humans, sparing some and striking others.

## An unbearable tragedy

I have witnessed many accidents both in the forces and in the civil aviation sector, including in my own company. On 3 March 2002, I received a call that hit me like a thunderbolt. A helicopter belonging to Deccan Aviation had crashed into a pond in the Krishna district of Andhra Pradesh. Everyone on board, including Lok Sabha Speaker G.M.C. Balayogi, was killed. The investigation report submitted six months after the accident by the Accident Investigation Committee to the Civil Aviation Ministry revealed that the pilot, Captain K.V. Menon, flew into thick fog with very poor visibility. He decided to do an emergency landing and wait for the fog to clear to resume his flight. But he mistook a twenty-acre shallow fish pond to be solid ground and descended. He realized his mistake too late – when he attempted a sudden take-off, the tail rotor hit the water and the chopper spun out of control and crashed. It was an unbearable tragedy. Captain Menon was an accomplished pilot who had flown extensively in Jammu and Kashmir over high altitudes, including over the forbidding heights of the Siachen Glacier and in inclement weather with terrorists lurking below. That he should die in peacetime on a regular flight in the plains along with a VIP passenger was hard to come to terms with.

The ill-fated flight with General Bipin Rawat on board was similarly flown by pilots of the IAF who had vast experience in flying over varied terrains and in all kinds of conditions. A tri-service inquiry headed by an air marshal has been ordered by the IAF into the incident. Nothing can be ruled out until all the evidence is gathered and technical and forensic investigation is completed. The report, when ready, should be widely disseminated so that future accidents can be prevented. Unfortunately, there are already conspiracy theories and fake videos circulating on social media, which do a lot of harm.

However these accidents are cautionary tales for pilots, engineers and ground-handling staff. Most flight-related accidents in the world are caused by pilot error and faulty maintenance. Disregarding standard operating procedures and throwing caution to the wind when undertaking flights in inclement weather or while under pressure causes such accidents.

It is well known now that there was thick fog on the day of the flight. There are some troubling questions that the investigation team may look into. Why was there no advance pilot helicopter before General Rawat's flight was cleared? For a VIP of his stature, a helicopter could have flown in advance and returned to advise cancellation of the flight if the fog was impenetrable.

## Handling pressure

It is not uncommon for VIPs to put pressure on pilots to take them to attend important functions. Sometimes, there is also pressure from the management of the organizations on the crew to undertake flights to please the VIP, or commercial pressure in the case of the private sector. And at times, the pilots themselves are at fault as they want to live up to their reputation of being daring.

Since many accidents occur in the mountains, especially during foul weather, it is pertinent to mention that low-ground fog and low clouds greatly hinder visibility. And as pilots fly visually and do not rely on instruments, in remote locations they have a tendency to cling closer to the ground to gain visibility. In these cases, there is spatial disorientation and greater danger of hitting an obstacle during landing and take-off. This may not have been the case in General Rawat's flight, but it bears emphasis nevertheless that pilots must not succumb to pressure or yield to the temptations of adventurism. They must have the courage to call off a flight if, in their opinion, it is unsafe to fly. The VIP and the commands in defence and civil management must show grace and prudence and not belittle or punish the pilot who says 'no'. Discretion is the better part of valour.

*The Hindu*, December 2021

# Acknowledgments

Grateful thanks to all the media outlets who afforded me a platform to share my views and stories. All views are my personal views and are not reflections of the original publishers of the articles. I am beholden to Gopalkrishna Gandhi, for writing a lovely foreword for *Our India*. T.N. Ninan, for writing an apt introduction and setting the tone for the rest of the book. Heartfelt thanks to Nandan Nilekani, Kiran Mazumdar-Shaw, T.V. Mohandas Pai and Kunal Basu for their kind words about the book. Finally, but most importantly, the readers who have nourished me, without whom a writer loses his sap and sustenance.

# About the Author

Captain G.R. Gopinath is the founder of Air Deccan, a retired army man, an award-winning farmer, an activist and the author of *Simply Fly: A Deccan Odyssey* and *You Cannot Miss This Flight: Essays on Emerging India.*